Math

GRADE 1

Fundamentals

Writing: Marti Beeck
Content Editing: Lisa Vitarisi Mathews
Copy Editing: Cathy Harber
　　　　　　　Laurie Westrich
Art Direction: Yuki Meyer
Cover Design: Yuki Meyer
Art Manager: Kathy Kopp
Illustration: Ann Iosa
Design/Production: Yuki Meyer
　　　　　　　　　Jessica Onken

EMC 3081

Evan-Moor®

Visit
teaching-standards.com
to view a correlation
of this book.
This is a free service.

**Correlated to
Current Standards**

**Congratulations on your purchase of some of the
finest teaching materials in the world.**

*Photocopying the pages in this book
is permitted for <u>single-classroom use only</u>.
Making photocopies for additional classes
or schools is prohibited.*

CPSIA: McNaughton & Gunn, Saline, MI USA [10/2021]

Contents

* This unit provides foundational practice for a related grade 2 Common Core State Standard.

What's in This Book

Math Fundamentals is your comprehensive resource for grade-level problem-solving and analysis practice. The broad scope of math skills ranges in difficulty on skill practice pages, allowing you to precisely target specific skills for each student.

- Each unit in this book corresponds to a Common Core cluster (the bold statements within a domain). The units are in the same order as the Common Core State Standards for easy reference; however, **the order does not suggest a teaching path**. (See page 8 for a suggested teaching path.)

- Each unit is divided into concept sections that include a student reference page showing multiple strategies and models, skill practice pages that progress from foundational to challenging, and a culminating problem-solving activity. These activities offer opportunities to investigate and analyze the concept, improve computational fluency, and apply the skill in student-friendly real-world contexts.

- The student pages may be assigned as individual practice or homework. They can also be used for small-group work or a whole-class lesson.

Teacher Page

Unit Overview

This page shows at a glance the concepts, skills, and mathematical practices in the unit.

Common Core State Standards information
The Common Core wording of the domain, cluster, and standards is provided, along with their codes.

Mathematical practices in the unit
This section lists the practices that students will use in the unit, along with the specific page numbers for each practice.

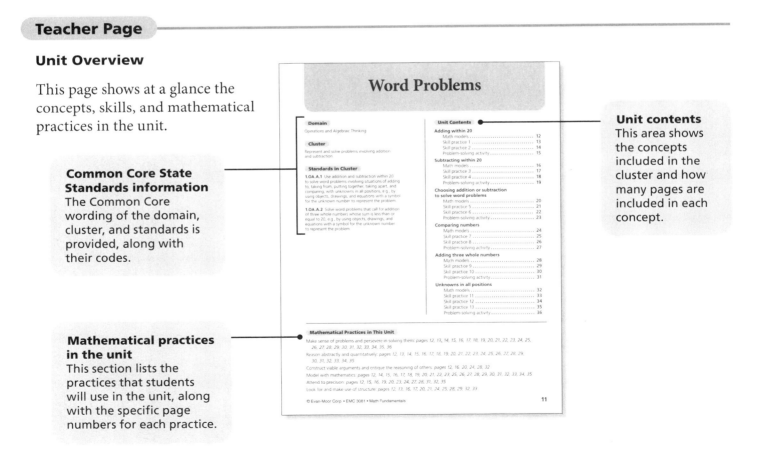

Unit contents
This area shows the concepts included in the cluster and how many pages are included in each concept.

Student Pages

Math Models

These reference pages help students with each concept.

Multiple solving strategies with examples
Several example problems are shown, along with all work and answers so students can follow the steps. Multiple strategies or models are used so students can choose what best fits their thinking or the type of problem.

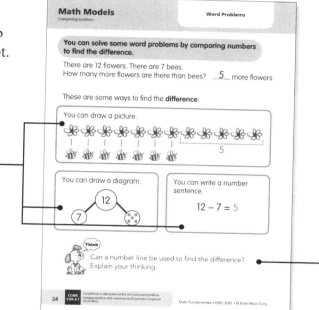

Reference page with many uses
- Introduce students to the types of problems they'll encounter.
- Print, project, or post it for reference as you teach the unit.
- Send it home as a resource for homework so parents can connect what they know with current methodology.

"Think" questions
"Think" questions help students apply what they have learned to a similar problem. The questions provide students an opportunity to talk about math strategies and to explain their thinking.

Skill Practice

These pages help students analyze concepts, gain fluency, and apply skills.

Example problem
The first skill practice page in each section includes an example to show students how to mark the answer and show their work.

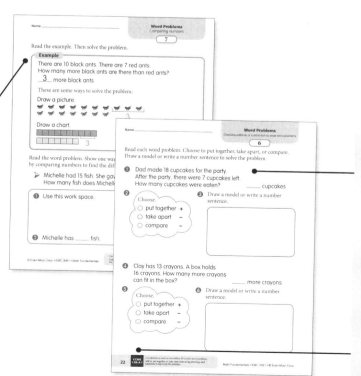

Practice problems
Students practice math skills and work toward fluency.

Standard identifier
This indicates the specific skill within the cluster, along with its Common Core Math Standard code (includes a letter designating the cluster).

Student Pages, *continued*

Problem-Solving Activity

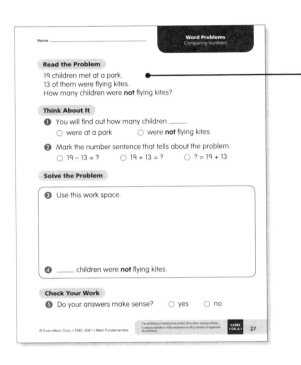

Real-world problem
Students tackle a real-world problem. The activity leads students through unpacking the problem: analyzing what the problem asks for, figuring out what information is needed to calculate the answer, showing their work or model, arriving at a solution, and checking their work.

Answer Key

Correct Answers or Examples

The correct response or an exemplar response is shown on a reduced version of the actual page.

Teachers may establish their own criteria for evaluating and scoring work shown leading to an answer.

Math Models

Small-Group Instruction

The Math Models pages are intended to be used in a small-group instruction setting. Consider the following approach:

1. Read aloud the concept statement to students.

2. Guide students through each example. Lead them in a discussion about the strategies.

3. Read aloud and discuss the "Think" question at the bottom of the page. Encourage students to participate in the discussion and explain their thinking. This is an opportunity for you to check students' understanding of the math concept.

The models included are suggestions. A variety of widely used models are represented in the book, but feel free to add additional models or integrate those used in class. Where counters are pictured, you may have students use actual manipulative counters or work with representations of them, as you see fit.

Parent Education

Send home Math Models pages for parent education.

Many parents may have questions about the new math strategies their children are learning. The math models will help them better understand the concepts so they can support their children's math education.

Suggested Teaching Path

If you wish to use this book as a core resource, we suggest using the units in the following order:

Math Fundamentals • EMC 3081 • © Evan-Moor Corp.

Strategies for Solving
Word Problems and Activities

1 **Read**  **or listen to** **the problem** carefully. Think about what it says.

2 **Draw** **a model** of the problem. It can be a picture, a diagram, or a chart of data.

3 **Think about** **what you need** to do to solve it.

Do you need to:

- add or subtract ?

- skip count **2, 4, 6** ?

- measure something?

- write an equation?

- figure out a piece of information before you solve the problem?

4 **Solve** **the problem.** Hint: Sometimes it will take two steps.

5 **Check** **your work.** Does your answer make sense?

Use *Math Fundamentals* to Reteach and Reinforce

The perfect companion to Evan-Moor's *Daily Math Practice*

Thousands of grade 1 through 6 classrooms use *Daily Math Practice* for focused practice and review. Multiple studies show that this type of distributed, or spaced, practice is a powerful strategy for achieving proficiency and retention of skills.

Student responses on the *Daily Math Practice* items will indicate which skills need additional practice or remediation. Use *Math Fundamentals* to provide the reteaching and additional practice. For example:

A student makes errors in week 24 of *Daily Math Practice*. Your assessment is that the student needs more practice with these skills.

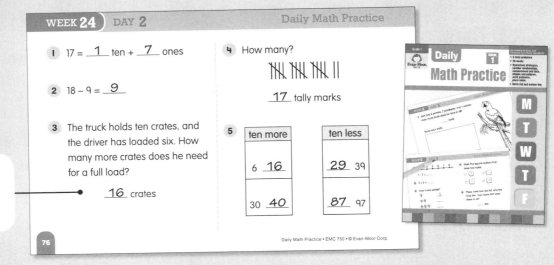

The student does not know whether to add or subtract.

Use these pages from *Math Fundamentals* to reteach and practice the skills the student has not mastered.

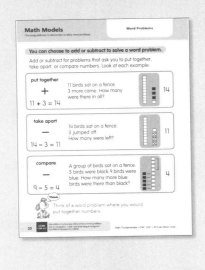

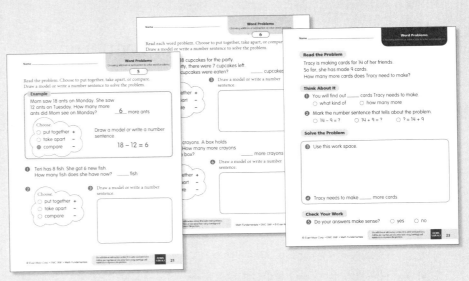

Word Problems

Domain

Operations and Algebraic Thinking

Cluster

Represent and solve problems involving addition and subtraction.

Standards in Cluster

1.OA.A.1 Use addition and subtraction within 20 to solve word problems involving situations of adding to, taking from, putting together, taking apart, and comparing, with unknowns in all positions, e.g., by using objects, drawings, and equations with a symbol for the unknown number to represent the problem.

1.OA.A.2 Solve word problems that call for addition of three whole numbers whose sum is less than or equal to 20, e.g., by using objects, drawings, and equations with a symbol for the unknown number to represent the problem.

Mathematical Practices in This Unit

Make sense of problems and persevere in solving them: *pages 12, 13, 14, 15, 16, 17, 18, 19, 20, 21, 22, 23, 24, 25, 26, 27, 28, 29, 30, 31, 32, 33, 34, 35, 36*

Reason abstractly and quantitatively: *pages 12, 13, 14, 15, 16, 17, 18, 19, 20, 21, 22, 23, 24, 25, 26, 27, 28, 29, 30, 31, 32, 33, 34, 35*

Construct viable arguments and critique the reasoning of others: *pages 12, 16, 20, 24, 28, 32*

Model with mathematics: *pages 12, 14, 15, 16, 17, 18, 19, 20, 21, 22, 23, 25, 26, 27, 28, 29, 30, 31, 32, 33, 34, 35*

Attend to precision: *pages 12, 15, 16, 19, 20, 23, 24, 27, 28, 31, 32, 35*

Look for and make use of structure: *pages 12, 13, 16, 17, 20, 21, 24, 25, 28, 29, 32, 33*

You can solve some word problems with addition.

Dan has 8 white socks and 2 gray socks.
How many socks does he have in all?   __10__ socks

These are some ways you can **put together** numbers:

You can draw a picture.

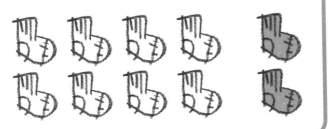

You can use counters.

You can draw a diagram.

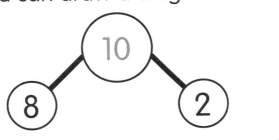

You can write a number sentence.

$$8 + 2 = 10$$

Think

Jesse solved the word problem. He wrote **8 + 2 = 10**.
Do you agree? Explain your thinking.

CCMS 1.OA.A.1 Use addition within 20 to solve word problems.
Add to or put together using objects, drawings, and equations
to represent the problem.

Math Fundamentals • EMC 3081 • © Evan-Moor Corp.

Read the example. Then solve the problem.

Example

6 ants sat on a log.
4 more ants came.
How many ants were there in all? ___**10**___ ants

These are some ways to solve the problem:

Draw a picture.	Draw a diagram.	Write a number sentence.
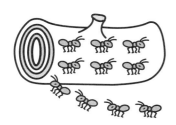	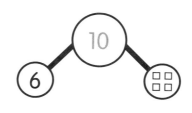	$6 + 4 = ?$

Read the word problem.
Show one way to solve the problem by adding.

➤ Luis has 8 fish. Tia has 7 fish.
How many fish do they have in all?

1 Use this work space.

2 They have _____ fish in all.

Use addition within 20 to solve word problems.
Add to or put together using objects, drawings, and equations
to represent the problem.

**CCMS
1.OA.A.1** 13

Name _____

Read each word problem.
Show one way to solve each problem by adding.

➤ There were 3 girls and 9 boys at Emma's party.
How many children were at the party?

1 Use this work space.

2 _____ children were at the party.

➤ Liz had 10 crayons. I gave her 5 more.
How many crayons does Liz have now?

3 Use this work space.

4 Liz has _____ crayons.

CCMS
1.OA.A.1
Use addition within 20 to solve word problems.
Add to or put together using objects, drawings, and equations
to represent the problem.

Math Fundamentals • EMC 3081 • © Evan-Moor Corp.

Read the Problem

Lily saw children flying kites at the park.
She counted 6 yellow and 7 blue kites.
How many kites did she see altogether?

Think About It

1 You will find out how many _____ Lily saw.

○ children   ○ parks   ○ kites

2 Mark the number sentence that tells about the problem.

○ $7 - 6 = ?$ ○ $6 + 7 = ?$ ○ $6 + ? = 7$

Solve the Problem

3 Use this work space.

4 Lily saw _____ kites altogether.

Check Your Work

5 Do your answers make sense?   ○ yes   ○ no

Use addition within 20 to solve word problems.
Add to or put together using objects, drawings, and equations
to represent the problem.

CCMS
1.OA.A.1

Math Models

Subtracting within 20

You can solve some word problems with subtraction.

15 apples were in the tree.
Jen picked 5 apples.
How many apples were left?   __10__ apples

These are some ways you can **take apart** numbers:

You can draw a picture.

You can use counters.

You can draw a diagram.

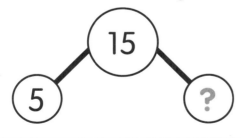

You can write a number sentence.

$$15 - 5 = ?$$

Think

What is your favorite math model to use for this problem? Explain your answer.

CCMS 1.OA.A.1 Use subtraction within 20 to solve word problems. Take away from or take apart using objects, drawings, and equations to represent the problem.

Math Fundamentals • EMC 3081 • © Evan-Moor Corp.

Read the example. Then solve the problem.

Example

10 ants sat on a log.
4 ants went away.
How many ants were left? __6__ ants

These are some ways to solve the problem:

Draw a picture.	Draw a diagram.	Write a number sentence.
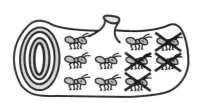	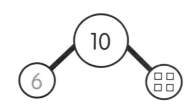	$10 - 4 = 6$

Read the word problem.
Show one way to solve the problem by subtracting.

➤ Mike had 15 fish. He gave 7 fish to Jan.
How many fish does Mike have now?

❶ Use this work space.

❷ Mike has _____ fish.

Use subtraction within 20 to solve word problems.
Take away from or take apart using objects, drawings,
and equations to represent the problem.

CCMS
1.0A.A.1

Read each word problem.
Show one way to solve each problem by subtracting.

➤ There were 12 children at Alisa's party. 9 children played games. How many children did **not** play games?

1 Use this work space.

2 _____ children did **not** play games.

➤ Carlos had 15 crayons. He lost 2 crayons. How many crayons does Carlos have left?

3 Use this work space.

4 Carlos has _____ crayons left.

CCMS 1.OA.A.1 Use subtraction within 20 to solve word problems. Take away from or take apart using objects, drawings, and equations to represent the problem.

Read the Problem

At the park, Harold saw 13 kites flying.
Then 3 kites got stuck in trees.
How many kites were still flying?

Think About It

1 You will find out how many _____ were still flying.
  ○ kites   ○ trees   ○ birds

2 Mark the number sentence that tells about the problem.
  ○ ? – 13 = 3   ○ 13 + 3 = ?   ○ 13 – 3 = ?

Solve the Problem

3 Use this work space.

4 _____ kites were still flying.

Check Your Work

5 Do your answers make sense?   ○ yes   ○ no

Use subtraction within 20 to solve word problems.
Take away from or take apart using objects, drawings,
and equations to represent the problem.

Math Models

Choosing addition or subtraction to solve word problems

You can choose to add or subtract to solve a word problem.

Add or subtract for problems that ask you to put together, take apart, or compare numbers. Look at each example:

put together

$+$

11 birds sat on a fence. 3 more came. How many were there in all?

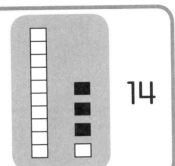

14

$11 + 3 = 14$

take apart

$-$

14 birds sat on a fence. 3 jumped off. How many were left?

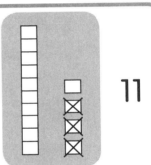

11

$14 - 3 = 11$

compare

$-$

A group of birds sat on a fence. 5 birds were black. 9 birds were blue. How many more blue birds were there than black?

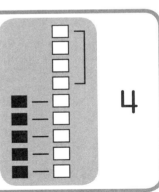

4

$9 - 5 = 4$

Think

Think of a word problem where you would put together numbers.

CCMS 1.0A.A.1 Use addition or subtraction within 20 to solve word problems. Add to, put together, or take away from using drawings and equations to represent the problem.

Math Fundamentals • EMC 3081 • © Evan-Moor Corp.

Read the problem. Choose to put together, take apart, or compare.
Draw a model or write a number sentence to solve the problem.

Example

Mom saw 18 ants on Monday. She saw
12 ants on Tuesday. How many more
ants did Mom see on Monday?   ___6___ more ants

Choose.

○ put together **+**

○ take apart   **–**

● compare   **–**

Draw a model or write a number sentence.

$$18 - 12 = 6$$

1 Teri has 8 fish. She got 6 new fish.
How many fish does she have now?   _____ fish

2

Choose.

○ put together **+**

○ take apart   **–**

○ compare   **–**

3 Draw a model or write a number sentence.

Use addition or subtraction within 20 to solve word problems.
Add to, put together, or take away from using drawings and
equations to represent the problem.

CCMS
1.OA.A.1

Read each word problem. Choose to put together, take apart, or compare.
Draw a model or write a number sentence to solve the problem.

1 Dad made 18 cupcakes for the party.
After the party, there were 7 cupcakes left.
How many cupcakes were eaten? _____ cupcakes

2
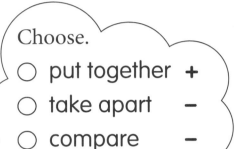
Choose.
○ put together **+**
○ take apart **–**
○ compare **–**

3 Draw a model or write a number sentence.

4 Clay has 13 crayons. A box holds
16 crayons. How many more crayons
can fit in the box? _____ more crayons

5
Choose.
○ put together **+**
○ take apart **–**
○ compare **–**

6 Draw a model or write a number sentence.

CCMS
1.OA.A.1 Use addition or subtraction within 20 to solve word problems.
Add to, put together, or take away from using drawings and
equations to represent the problem.

Math Fundamentals • EMC 3081 • © Evan-Moor Corp.

Name _____

Read the Problem

Tracy is making cards for 14 of her friends.
So far, she has made 9 cards.
How many more cards does Tracy need to make?

Think About It

1 You will find out _____ cards Tracy needs to make.
  ○ what kind of   ○ how many more

2 Mark the number sentence that tells about the problem.
  ○ $14 - 9 = ?$ ○ $14 + 9 = ?$ ○ $? = 14 + 9$

Solve the Problem

3 Use this work space.

4 Tracy needs to make _____ more cards.

Check Your Work

5 Do your answers make sense?   ○ yes   ○ no

Use addition or subtraction within 20 to solve word problems.
Add to, put together, or take away from using drawings and
equations to represent the problem.

**CCMS
1.OA.A.1**

Math Models
Comparing numbers

You can solve some word problems by comparing numbers to find the difference.

There are 12 flowers. There are 7 bees.
How many more flowers are there than bees?   __5__ more flowers

These are some ways to find the **difference**:

You can draw a picture.

5

You can draw a diagram.

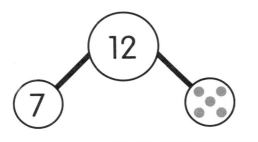

You can write a number sentence.

$$12 - 7 = 5$$

Think

Can a number line be used to find the difference?
Explain your thinking.

CCMS 1.0A.A.1 Use addition or subtraction within 20 to solve word problems. Compare numbers with unknowns in all positions to represent the problem.

Math Fundamentals • EMC 3081 • © Evan-Moor Corp.

Read the example. Then solve the problem.

Example

There are 10 black ants. There are 7 red ants.
How many more black ants are there than red ants?

___3___ more black ants

These are some ways to solve the problem:

Draw a picture.

3

Draw a chart.

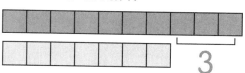
3

Write a number sentence.

10 – 7 = 3

Read the word problem. Show one way to solve the problem
by comparing numbers to find the difference.

➤ Michelle had 15 fish. She gave 7 fish to Tan.
How many fish does Michelle have now?

1 Use this work space.

2 Michelle has _____ fish.

Use addition or subtraction within 20 to solve word problems.
Compare numbers with unknowns in all positions to represent
the problem.

CCMS
1.0A.A.1

25

Read each word problem. Show one way to solve each problem by comparing numbers to find the difference.

➤ At Keisha's party, 4 children ate cake. 8 children ate pie. How many more children ate pie than cake?

1 Use this work space.

2 _____ more children ate pie.

➤ Meg has 20 crayons. Liza has 13 crayons. How many fewer crayons does Liza have?

3 Use this work space.

4 Liza has _____ fewer crayons.

CCMS 1.0A.A.1 Use addition or subtraction within 20 to solve word problems. Compare numbers with unknowns in all positions to represent the problem.

Math Fundamentals • EMC 3081 • © Evan-Moor Corp.

Read the Problem

19 children met at a park.
13 of them were flying kites.
How many children were **not** flying kites?

Think About It

1 You will find out how many children _____.

○ were at a park   ○ were **not** flying kites

2 Mark the number sentence that tells about the problem.

○ 19 – 13 = ?   ○ 19 + 13 = ?   ○ ? = 19 + 13

Solve the Problem

3 Use this work space.

4 _____ children were **not** flying kites.

Check Your Work

5 Do your answers make sense?   ○ yes   ○ no

Use addition or subtraction within 20 to solve word problems.
Compare numbers with unknowns in all positions to represent
the problem.

CCMS
1.OA.A.1

27

You can solve some word problems by adding three numbers.

Carla went to a farm.
She saw 5 cows, 6 goats, and 2 horses.
How many animals did she see?   ___13___ animals

These are some ways to add three numbers:

You can use counters.

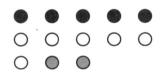

You can draw a diagram.

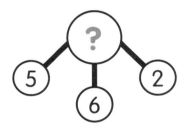

You can write a number sentence.

$$5 + 6 + 2 = ?$$

$$11 + 2 = 13$$

Think

Explain some ways to choose which numbers
to add first.

CCMS 1.OA.A.1 Solve word problems that call for adding three whole numbers.
Use objects, drawings, and equations with a symbol for the
unknown number to represent the problem.

Math Fundamentals • EMC 3081 • © Evan-Moor Corp.

Read the example. Then solve the problem.

> **Example**
>
> Leon saw 3 ants in the garden. He saw 7 ants in the grass. He saw 5 ants in the dirt. How many ants did Leon see?
>
> ___15___ ants
>
> These are some ways to solve the problem:
>
> | Use counters. | Draw a diagram. | Write a number sentence. |
> |---|---|---|
> | 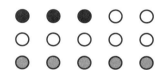 | 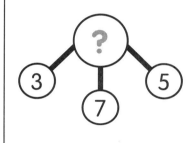 | $3 + 7 + 5 = ?$
 $10 + 5 = ?$
 $10 + 5 = 15$ |

Read the word problem.
Show one way to solve the problem by adding three numbers.

➤ Tina has many pet fish. She has 4 striped, 8 blue, and 2 gray fish. How many fish does Tina have altogether?

> **1** Use this work space.
>
>
>
>
>
>
> **2** Tina has _____ fish altogether.

Solve word problems that call for adding three whole numbers. Use objects, drawings, and equations with a symbol for the unknown number to represent the problem.

CCMS
1.0A.A.1

Name _____

Read each word problem.
Show one way to solve each problem by adding three numbers.

➤ Caleb went to Emma's party. He saw 1 red, 6 blue, and 6 green balloons. How many balloons did Caleb see?

1 Use this work space.

2 Caleb saw _____ balloons.

➤ Melita found 3 old boxes of crayons. The first box had 7 crayons. The second box had 8 crayons. The third box had 5 crayons. How many crayons did Melita find?

3 Use this work space.

4 Melita found _____ crayons.

CCMS
1.OA.A.1 Solve word problems that call for adding three whole numbers. Use objects, drawings, and equations with a symbol for the unknown number to represent the problem.

Math Fundamentals • EMC 3081 • © Evan-Moor Corp.

Name _____

Read the Problem

Lisa and her dad rode their bikes 5 blocks to buy a book. Next, they rode 2 more blocks to the park. Then they rode 7 blocks back home. How many blocks did they ride?

Think About It

1 You will find out how many _____.

○ parks they saw   ○ blocks they rode

2 Mark the number sentence that tells about the problem.

○ 5 + 2 + ? = 7   ○ 5 + 2 + 7 = ?   ○ 7 – 2 – 5 = ?

Solve the Problem

3 Use this work space.

4 Lisa and her dad rode _____ blocks.

Check Your Work

5 Do your answers make sense?   ○ yes   ○ no

Solve word problems that call for adding three whole numbers. Use objects, drawings, and equations with a symbol for the unknown number to represent the problem.

CCMS 1.0A.A.1   31

Math Models

Unknowns in all positions

> You can use a symbol to stand for an unknown number in a number sentence. The symbol can be in different places.

There were 19 bugs.
A bird ate 6 of them.
How many bugs were left? ___13___ bugs

These are some ways to write a number sentence to help you solve the problem:

Kim

I wrote $19 - 6 = \,?$
bugs   eaten   unknown
in all

Ben

I wrote $6 + \,? = 19$
eaten unknown bugs
in all

Juana

I wrote $? = 19 - 6$
unknown bugs   eaten
in all

Think

Explain how Kim, Ben, and Juana might tell about each number sentence. What models could they use?

Read the example. Then solve the problem.

Example

17 ants went walking.
It started to rain.
10 ants ran under a rock.
How many ants were still walking? ___7___ ants

(17 – ? = 10)   (17 – 10 = ?)   (? = 17 – 10)

Read the word problem. Use **?** as the unknown number.
Write 3 number sentences that can help you solve the problem.

1 Adam has 14 pet fish.
8 of his fish swim together in a group.
How many fish do **not** swim in the group? _____ fish

2

3

4

© Evan-Moor Corp. • EMC 3081 • Math Fundamentals

Use addition and subtraction within 20 to solve word problems.
Show situations with unknowns in all positions.

CCMS
1.OA.A.1 **33**

Read each word problem. Use **?** as the unknown number.
Write 3 number sentences that can help you solve the problem.

1 At Jessica's party, 7 children sang songs. 6 children danced.

How many children sang and danced?   _____ children

2

3

4

---

5 A small box has 8 crayons. A bigger box has 16 crayons.

How many fewer crayons are in the small box?   _____ fewer
crayons

6

7

8

 CCMS
1.0A.A.1 Use addition and subtraction within 20 to solve word problems.
Show situations with unknowns in all positions.

Math Fundamentals • EMC 3081 • © Evan-Moor Corp.

Read each word problem. Use **?** as the unknown number.
Write 3 number sentences that can help you solve the problem.

1 My dog Gus had 14 bones. He hid 6 of them.

How many bones were **not** hidden? _____ bones

2

3

4

---

5 At the park, Tami jumped 15 times. Pat did 3 more jumps

than Tami. How many jumps did Pat do? _____ jumps

6

7

8

Use addition and subtraction within 20 to solve word problems.
Show situations with unknowns in all positions.

**CCMS
1.0A.A.1** 35

Read the Problem

Ed went to the park 15 times in May. He went 8 times with Dad. The other times he went with Mom.
How many times did Ed go to the park with Mom?

Think About It

1 You will find out how many times Ed went to the park _____.

○ with Dad　　○ with Mom　　○ in a car

2 Mark the number sentence that tells about the problem.

○ 8 − 15 = ?　　○ 15 + 8 = ?　　○ ? = 15 − 8

Solve the Problem

3 Use this work space.

4 Ed went to the park _____ times with Mom.

Check Your Work

5 Do your answers make sense?　　○ yes　　○ no

CCMS
1.OA.A.1 Use addition and subtraction within 20 to solve word problems. Show situations with unknowns in all positions.

Math Fundamentals • EMC 3081 • © Evan-Moor Corp.

Operations and Number Relationships

Domain

Operations and Algebraic Thinking

Cluster

Understand and apply properties of operations and the relationship between addition and subtraction.

Standards in Cluster

1.OA.B.3 Apply properties of operations as strategies to add and subtract. Examples: If 8 + 3 = 11 is known, then 3 + 8 = 11 is also known (commutative property of addition). To add 2 + 6 + 4, the second two numbers can be added to make a ten, so 2 + 6 + 4 = 2 + 10 = 12 (associative property of addition).

1.OA.B.4 Understand subtraction as an unknown-addend problem. For example, subtract 10 − 8 by finding the number that makes 10 when added to 8.

Unit Contents

Mathematical Practices in This Unit

Make sense of problems and persevere in solving them: *pages 41, 45, 50*

Reason abstractly and quantitatively: *pages 39, 40, 41, 42, 43, 44, 45, 47, 48, 49, 50*

Construct viable arguments and critique the reasoning of others: *pages 38, 42, 46*

Model with mathematics: *pages 38, 41, 42, 45, 50*

Attend to precision: *pages 41, 45, 50*

Look for and make use of structure: *pages 39, 40, 43, 44, 47, 48*

Math Models

Commutative property

You can change the order of addends.

If you know that 5 + 8 = 13, then you also know that 8 + 5 = 13.

This is one way to show how the order can be changed:

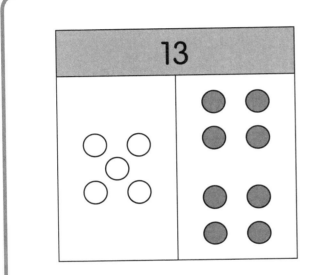

5 + 8 = 13

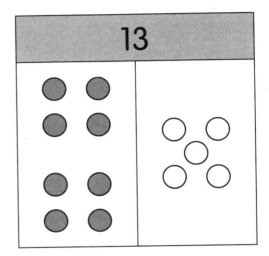

8 + 5 = 13

Think

Explain another type of model you could use to show **5 + 8 = 13** and **8 + 5 = 13**.

CCMS 1.OA.B.3 Apply properties of operations to add (commutative property).

Add. Write a new number sentence by changing the order of the addends.

Example

Add.

$7 + 3 = \underline{10}$

Change the order.

$3 + 7 = \underline{10}$

Add	Change the Order
1 $4 + 12 = \underline{\hspace{1cm}}$	$\underline{12} + \underline{4} = \underline{16}$
2 $10 + 7 = \underline{\hspace{1cm}}$	$\underline{\hspace{1cm}} + \underline{\hspace{1cm}} = \underline{\hspace{1cm}}$
3 $5 + 11 = \underline{\hspace{1cm}}$	$\underline{\hspace{1cm}} + \underline{\hspace{1cm}} = \underline{\hspace{1cm}}$
4 $80 + 1 = \underline{\hspace{1cm}}$	$\underline{\hspace{1cm}} + \underline{\hspace{1cm}} = \underline{\hspace{1cm}}$

Add. Then write a new number sentence by changing
the order of the addends.

❶ If 10 + 6 = ___, then _6_ + _10_ = _16_.

_____

❷ If 7 + 8 = ___, then ___ + ___ = ___.

_____

❸ If 9 + 4 = ___, then ___ + ___ = ___.

_____

❹ If 17 + 3 = ___, then ___ + ___ = ___.

_____

❺ If 1 + 69 = ___, then ___ + ___ = ___.

_____

❻ If 100 + 10 = ___, then ___ + ___ = ___.

Name _____

Read the Problem

Carl has 8 blue socks and 4 white socks.
Ali has 4 blue socks and 8 white socks.
How many socks does Carl have?
How many socks does Ali have?

Think About It

1 You will find out how many socks Carl and Ali have _____.

○ altogether   ○ each   ○ left over

2 Mark the **two** number sentences that have the same sum.

○ $8 + 4 = ?$ ○ $8 + 8 = ?$ ○ $4 + 8 = ?$

Solve the Problem

3 Use this work space.

4 Carl has _____ socks.

5 Ali has _____ socks.

Check Your Work

6 Do your answers make sense?   ○ yes   ○ no

When you add three or more numbers, you can change the grouping.

$$4 + 1 + 5 = 10$$

These are some ways to show how grouping can be changed:

a

$$(4 + 1) + 5 = 10$$
$$5 + 5 = 10$$

b

$$4 + (1 + 5) = 10$$
$$4 + 6 = 10$$

c

$$4 + 1 + 5 = 10$$
$$1 + 9 = 10$$

Think

Look at **a**, **b**, **c**. Explain which grouping you would choose to solve this problem.

42

CCMS 1.OA.B.3 Apply properties of operations to add (associative property).

Math Fundamentals • EMC 3081 • © Evan-Moor Corp.

Name _____

Add. Then add again in a different order.

Example

$(3 + 7) + 4 =$ __?__
$10 + 4 =$ __14__

$3 + (7 + 4) =$ __?__
$3 + 11 =$ __14__

❶ $5 + (10 + 2) =$ ____ $(5 + 10) + 2 =$ ____

❷ $(15 + 5) + 0 =$ ____ $15 + (5 + 0) =$ ____

❸ $20 + (5 + 5) =$ ____ $(20 + 5) + 5 =$ ____

❹ $(80 + 0) + 1 =$ ____ $80 + (0 + 1) =$ ____

Add. Draw a line around the numbers you chose to add first.

1 10 + (4 + 5) = ____

_____

2 7 + 3 + 7 = ____

_____

3 8 + 3 + 6 = ____

_____

4 9 + 1 + 5 = ____

_____

5 2 + 8 + 10 = ____

_____

6 20 + 10 + 30 = ____

CCMS
1.OA.B.3 Apply properties of operations to add (associative property).

Math Fundamentals • EMC 3081 • © Evan-Moor Corp.

Read the Problem

The kids saw 6 tigers, 4 bears, and 8 zebras at the zoo.
How many animals did the kids see?

Think About It

1 You will find out how many _____ were seen.

○ animals   ○ zoos   ○ lions

2 Mark the grouping you like best.

○ $(6 + 4) + 8 = ?$ ○ $6 + (4 + 8) = ?$ ○ $(6 + 8) + 4 = ?$

Solve the Problem

3 Use this work space.

4 The kids saw _____ animals.

Check Your Work

5 Do your answers make sense?   ○ yes   ○ no

Math Models

Using the unknown addend

You can solve a subtraction problem by finding the **unknown addend.**

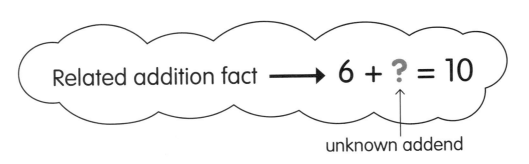

$$10 - 6 = \text{?} \longleftarrow \text{unknown addend}$$

Related addition fact $\longrightarrow 6 + \text{?} = 10$

unknown addend

These are two ways to find the **unknown addend**:

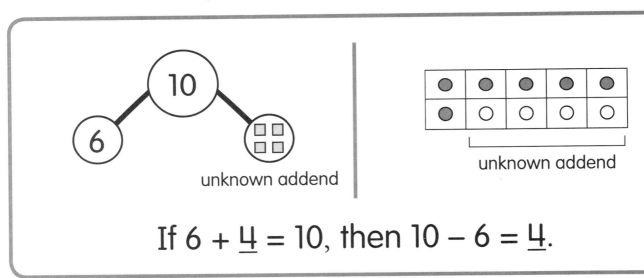

unknown addend

unknown addend

If $6 + \underline{4} = 10$, then $10 - 6 = \underline{4}$.

Think

Maya says that the number sentence **7 + 8 = 15** can help her solve **15 − ? = 7**. Do you agree? Explain your thinking.

CCMS 1.OA.B.4 Understand subtraction as an unknown-addend problem.   Math Fundamentals • EMC 3081 • © Evan-Moor Corp.

Find the unknown addend first. Then use the unknown addend to help you find the difference.

Example

First, add. $3 + \underline{10} = 13$

Then subtract. $13 - 3 = \underline{10}$

---

1 First, add.

$7 + \underline{\hphantom{00}} = 15$

Then subtract.

$15 - 7 = \underline{\hphantom{000}}$

3 First, add.

$\underline{\hphantom{00}} + 5 = 12$

Then subtract.

$12 - 5 = \underline{\hphantom{000}}$

---

2 First, add.

$\underline{\hphantom{00}} + 9 = 20$

Then subtract.

$20 - 9 = \underline{\hphantom{000}}$

4 First, add.

$10 + \underline{\hphantom{00}} = 40$

Then subtract.

$40 - 10 = \underline{\hphantom{000}}$

Find the unknown addend.
Use the unknown addend to help you find the difference.

1 Add. $7 + \underline{\quad} = 17$ Subtract. $17 - 7 = \underline{\quad}$

2 Add. $\underline{\quad} + 6 = 15$ Subtract. $15 - \underline{\quad} = 6$

3 Add. $11 + \underline{\quad} = 20$ Subtract. $20 - 11 = \underline{\quad}$

4 Add. $\underline{\quad} + 20 = 30$ Subtract. $30 - \underline{\quad} = 20$

5 Add. $20 + 80 = \underline{\quad}$ Subtract. $80 = 100 - \underline{\quad}$

CCMS 1.OA.B.4 Understand subtraction as an unknown-addend problem.

Math Fundamentals • EMC 3081 • © Evan-Moor Corp.

Mark the addition number sentence that can help you solve each subtraction number sentence. Then write the answer.

Example

$15 - 5 = \underline{10}$

○ $15 + 5 = 20$
● $10 + 5 = 15$

1 $21 - 1 = \underline{}$

○ $1 + 20 = 21$
○ $10 + 11 = 21$

2 $18 - 9 = \underline{}$

○ $9 + 9 = 18$
○ $6 + 3 = 9$

3 $14 - 8 = \underline{}$

○ $4 + 4 = 8$
○ $8 + 6 = 14$

4 $50 - 10 = \underline{}$

○ $50 + 10 = 60$
○ $10 + 40 = 50$

Read the Problem

Cam saw 13 books on the table. She put 6 of them away.
How many books were left on the table?

Think About It

1 Mark the subtraction number sentence that tells about the problem.

○ $6 - 3 = ?$ ○ $13 - 6 = ?$ ○ $31 - 6 = ?$

2 Mark the addition number sentence that can help you.

○ $13 + 6 = 19$ ○ $13 + 7 = 20$ ○ $6 + 7 = 13$

Solve the Problem

3 Use this work space.

4 _____ books were left on the table.

Check Your Work

5 Do your answers make sense? ○ yes ○ no

CCMS 1.OA.B.4 Understand subtraction as an unknown-addend problem.

Math Fundamentals • EMC 3081 • © Evan-Moor Corp.

Add and Subtract Within 20

Domain

Operations and Algebraic Thinking

Cluster

Add and subtract within 20.

Standards in Cluster

1.OA.C.5 Relate counting to addition and subtraction (e.g., by counting on 2 to add 2).

1.OA.C.6 Add and subtract within 20, demonstrating fluency for addition and subtraction within 10. Use strategies such as counting on; making ten (e.g., $8 + 6 = 8 + 2 + 4 = 10 + 4 = 14$); decomposing a number leading to a ten (e.g., $13 - 4 = 13 - 3 - 1 = 10 - 1 = 9$); using the relationship between addition and subtraction (e.g., knowing that $8 + 4 = 12$, one knows $12 - 8 = 4$); and creating equivalent but easier or known sums (e.g., adding $6 + 7$ by creating the known equivalent $6 + 6 + 1 = 12 + 1 = 13$).

Unit Contents

Mathematical Practices in This Unit

Make sense of problems and persevere in solving them: *pages 55, 59, 63, 67, 72*

Reason abstractly and quantitatively: *pages 52, 53, 54, 55, 56, 57, 58, 59, 60, 61, 62, 63, 64, 65, 66, 67, 68, 69, 70, 71, 72*

Construct viable arguments and critique the reasoning of others: *pages 52, 56, 60, 64, 68*

Model with mathematics: *pages 52, 53, 54, 55, 56, 57, 58, 59, 60, 61, 62, 63, 64, 65, 66, 67, 68, 69, 70, 71, 72*

Attend to precision: *pages 52, 53, 54, 55, 56, 57, 58, 59, 60, 61, 62, 63, 64, 65, 66, 67, 68, 69, 70, 71, 72*

Look for and make use of structure: *pages 52, 53, 56, 57, 60, 61, 64, 65, 68, 69*

You can count on to add small numbers such as **1, 2, or 3.**

$$11 + 3 = ?$$

These are some ways to **count on**:

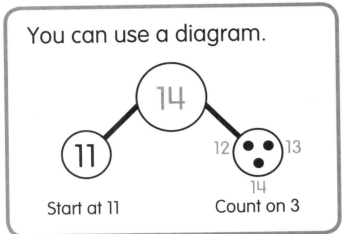

You can use a diagram.

14

11

12 13
14

Start at 11   Count on 3

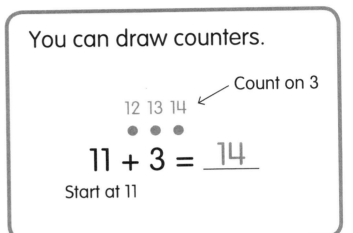

You can draw counters.

Count on 3

12 13 14
● ● ●

$$11 + 3 = \underline{14}$$

Start at 11

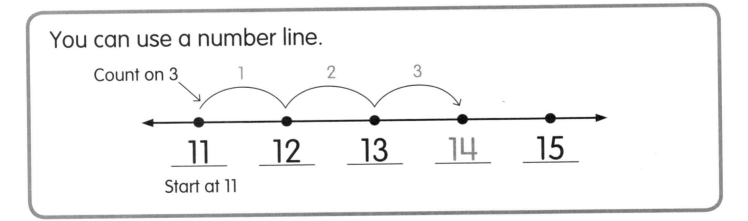

You can use a number line.

Count on 3   1   2   3

$\underline{11}$ $\underline{12}$ $\underline{13}$ $\underline{14}$ $\underline{15}$

Start at 11

Think

Kris wants to add **17 + 2 = ?** She made a number line that starts with **2.** Do you agree? Explain your thinking.

52 CCMS 1.0A.C.5 Relate counting to addition. Use counting on to add.

Math Fundamentals • EMC 3081 • © Evan-Moor Corp.

Name _____

Look at each number sentence. Show one way to solve with counting on.

Example

$$9 + 2 = \text{?}$$

Use a diagram.

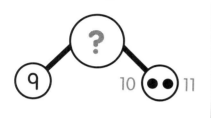

Draw counters.

10 11
• •

$9 + 2 = \underline{11}$

Use a number line.

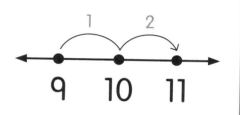

---

❶ $7 + 1 = \underline{\hspace{1cm}}$

❸ $10 + 2 = \underline{\hspace{1cm}}$

---

❷ $12 + 3 = \underline{\hspace{1cm}}$

❹ $2 + 14 = \underline{\hspace{1cm}}$

Relate counting to addition.
Use counting on to add.

Look at each number sentence. Show one way to solve with counting on.

❶ 8 + 3 = _____

❹ 6 + 3 = _____

❷ 2 + 17 = _____

❺ 13 + 1 = _____

❸ 15 + 1 = _____

❻ 18 + 2 = _____

CCMS
1.OA.C.5 Relate counting to addition.
Use counting on to add.

Read the Problem

Dad ate 7 grapes.
Then he ate 2 more.
How many grapes did Dad eat?

Think About It

1 You will find out how many grapes Dad _____.

○ picked   ○ gave away   ○ ate

2 To solve the problem, you will _____.

○ count on from 7   ○ count on from 2

Solve the Problem

3 Use this work space.

4 Dad ate _____ grapes.

Check Your Work

5 Do your answers make sense?   ○ yes   ○ no

Relate counting to addition.
Use counting on to add.

You can count back to subtract small numbers such as **1, 2, or 3**.

$$18 - 2 = ?$$

These are some ways to **count back**:

You can use a diagram.

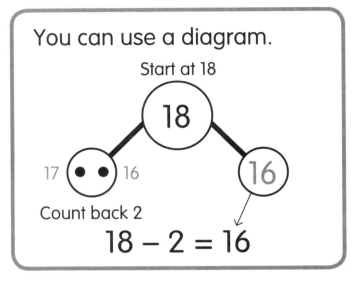

Start at 18

Count back 2

$$18 - 2 = 16$$

You can draw counters.

Count back 2

17 16

$$18 - 2 = \underline{16}$$

Start at 18

You can use a number line.

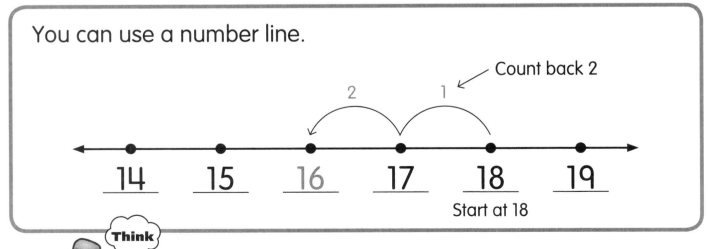

Count back 2

2   1

14   15   16   17   18   19

Start at 18

Think

Maria wants to solve **20 – 3 = ?** She counts back, saying, "**19, 18, 17**." Then she says, "I know that **20 – 3 = 17**!" Do you agree? Explain your thinking.

CCMS 1.OA.C.5 Relate counting to subtraction.

Math Fundamentals • EMC 3081 • © Evan-Moor Corp.

Look at each number sentence. Show one way to solve with counting back.

Example

$$8 - 3 = ?$$

Use a diagram.	Draw counters.	Use a number line.

Use a diagram.

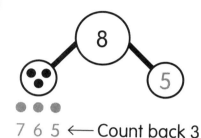

7 6 5 ← Count back 3

Draw counters.

Count back 3
7 6 5
● ● ●

$$8 - 3 = \underline{\ 5\ }$$

Use a number line.

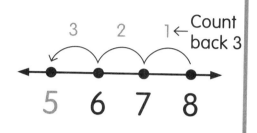

5 6 7 8

① $9 - 1 =$ _____

③ $11 - 2 =$ _____

② $15 - 3 =$ _____

④ $20 - 1 =$ _____

Look at each number sentence. Show one way to solve with counting back.

1 12 − 1 = ____

4 13 − 2 = ____

2 18 − 3 = ____

5 16 − 1 = ____

3 14 − 2 = ____

6 17 − 3 = ____

CCMS
1.OA.C.5 Relate counting to subtraction.

Name _____

Read the Problem

Jan had 12 pencils.
She gave 2 pencils to Kai.
How many pencils did Jan have left?

Think About It

1 You will find out how many pencils Jan _____.

○ gave to Kai   ○ had left   ○ will get

2 To solve the problem, you will _____.

○ count back from 2   ○ count back from 12

Solve the Problem

3 Use this work space.

4 Jan had _____ pencils left.

Check Your Work

5 Do your answers make sense?   ○ yes   ○ no

> **You can make a ten to help you add.**

$$4 + 7 = ?$$

These are two ways to **make a ten**:

Use a ten frame.

$$(4 + 6) + 1 = 11$$

$$4 + 7 = 11$$

Draw a chart.

$$4 + 7 = ?$$

$$1 + (3 + 7) = ?$$
$$10$$

$$1 + 10 = 11$$

Think

How can you make a ten to solve **11 + 5**?
Explain your thinking. Draw your answer below.

Look at each number sentence. Show one way to solve by making a ten.

Example

$8 + 5 = ?$

Use a ten frame.

$8 + 5 = ?$
$(8 + 2) + 3 = 13$

Draw a chart.

$8 + 5 = ?$
$(8 + 2) + 3 = 13$
10

❶ $6 + 7 = $ _____

❸ $7 + 8 = $ _____

❷ $9 + 4 = $ _____

❹ $5 + 11 = $ _____

Look at each number sentence. Show one way to solve by making a ten.

1 5 + 9 = ____

4 12 + 7 = ____

2 6 + 5 = ____

5 8 + 9 = ____

3 11 + 3 = ____

6 13 + 6 = ____

CCMS 1.OA.C.6 Use making a ten as a strategy to add.

Name _____

Read the Problem

Ron likes hats.
He has 7 baseball caps.
He has 6 cowboy hats.
How many hats does Ron have?

Think About It

1 You will find out how many hats Ron _____.

　○ lost 　　　○ has 　　　○ gave away

2 Mark the number sentence that makes a ten to add.

　○ (7 + 3) + 3 　　　○ (7 + 4) + 2 　　　○ (7 + 5) + 1

Solve the Problem

3 Use this work space.

4 Ron has _____ hats.

Check Your Work

5 Do your answers make sense? 　　　○ yes 　　　○ no

Math Models
Leading to a ten

You can take a number apart, leading to a ten to help you subtract.

$$15 - 8 = ?$$

These are two ways to **lead to a ten**:

Use a ten frame.	Draw a chart.

Use a ten frame.

$$(15 - 5) - 3 = 7$$

$$15 - 8 = 7$$

Draw a chart.

$$15 - 8 = ?$$

$$(15 - 5) - 3 = ?$$
10

$$10 - 3 = 7$$

Think

If you solve **13 − 5**, how can you lead to a ten?
Explain your thinking.

CCMS 1.OA.C.6 Use decomposing a number leading to a ten to subtract.

Math Fundamentals • EMC 3081 • © Evan-Moor Corp.

Look at each number sentence. Show one way to lead to a ten to subtract.

Example

$$13 - 4 = ?$$

Use a ten frame.

$$(13 - 3) - 1 = 9$$
$$13 - 4 = 9$$

Draw a chart.

$$13 - 4 = ?$$

$$(13 - 3) - 1 = 9$$
10

$$10 - 1 = 9$$

❶ $12 - 5 =$ _____

❸ $11 - 3 =$ _____

❷ $15 - 6 =$ _____

❹ $14 - 9 =$ _____

Use decomposing a number leading to a ten to subtract.

Look at each number sentence. Show one way to subtract by leading to a ten.

1 13 – 7 = _____

4 16 – 7 = _____

2 17 – 8 = _____

5 11 – 4 = _____

3 15 – 9 = _____

6 12 – 4 = _____

CCMS
1.OA.C.6 Use decomposing a number leading to a ten to subtract.

Math Fundamentals • EMC 3081 • © Evan-Moor Corp.

Read the Problem

16 children were painting.
Then 9 of them went out to play.
How many children were still painting?

Think About It

1 You will find out how many children were _____.

○ still painting   ○ still playing   ○ painting outside

2 Mark the number sentence that leads to a ten.

○ $(16 - 4) - 5 = ?$ ○ $(16 - 5) - 4 = ?$ ○ $(16 - 6) - 3 = ?$

Solve the Problem

3 Use this work space.

4 _____ children were still painting.

Check Your Work

5 Do your answers make sense?   ○ yes   ○ no

Math Models

Using equivalent or known sums

You can use a math fact you already know to help you add or subtract.

These are some examples:

Use doubles + 1.

$$7 + 8 = \text{?}$$

I know $7 + 7 = 14$.
So, $7 + (7 + 1) = 15$.

$$7 + 8 = 15$$

Use an easier math fact.

$$7 + 9 = \text{?}$$

I know $7 + 10 = 17$.
So, $7 + (10 - 1) = 16$.

$$7 + 9 = 16$$

Think addition.

$$13 - 6 = \text{?}$$

I know $6 + 6 = 12$.
So, $6 + (6 + 1) = 13$.

$$13 - 6 = 7$$

Use an easier difference.

$$16 - 5 = \text{?}$$

I know $15 - 5 = 10$.
So, $(15 + 1) - 5 = 11$.

$$16 - 5 = 11$$

Think

Think of a math fact you already know that can help you solve **17 − 8 = ?** Explain your thinking.

68 CCMS 1.OA.C.6 Use equivalent or known sums to add or subtract.

Math Fundamentals • EMC 3081 • © Evan-Moor Corp.

Look at each number sentence. Use a math fact
that you already know to help you solve it.

Example

$9 + 8 = ?$

I know $10 + 8 = 18$.
So, $(10 - 1) + 8 = 17$.

$9 + 8 = \underline{\ 17\ }$

$14 - 8 = ?$

I know $14 - 7 = 7$.
So, $14 - (7 + 1) = 6$.

$14 - 8 = \underline{\ 6\ }$

❶ $6 + 7 = ?$

I know
So,

$6 + 7 = \underline{\ \ \ }$

❷ $15 - 9 = ?$

I know
So,

$15 - 9 = \underline{\ \ \ }$

Look at each number sentence. Use a math fact
that you already know to help you solve it.

1 $6 + 5 = ?$

I know $5 + 5 = 10$
So, $(5 + 1) + 5 = 11$

$6 + 5 = \underline{\hspace{1cm}}$

3 $14 - 6 = ?$

I know
So,

$14 - 6 = \underline{\hspace{1cm}}$

2 $9 + ? = 16$

I know
So,

$9 + \underline{\hspace{1cm}} = 16$

4 $19 - 8 = ?$

I know
So,

$19 - 8 = \underline{\hspace{1cm}}$

CCMS 1.OA.C.6 Use equivalent or known sums to add or subtract.

Write the missing number to complete each number sentence.
Mark the number sentence that can help you solve it.

Example

__6__ + 7 = 13

● 6 + 6 = 12
○ 13 + 7 = 20

❶ 15 – ____ = 8

○ 7 + 8 = 15
○ 7 + 1 = 8

❷ ____ + 9 = 17

○ 9 + 3 = 12
○ 8 + 8 = 16

❸ 5 + 6 = ____

○ 5 + 5 = 10
○ 5 + 1 = 6

❹ 20 – ____ = 9

○ 4 + 5 = 9
○ 10 + 10 = 20

Use equivalent or known sums to add or subtract.

CCMS
1.OA.C.6   71

Name _____

Read the Problem

Mom picked 12 apples.
She used 7 apples to make a pie.
How many apples were left?

Think About It

1 You will find out how many apples were _____.

○ used   ○ left   ○ picked

2 Mark **two** number sentences that can help you.

○ 12 + 7 = 19   ○ 6 + 6 = 12   ○ 12 − 6 = 6

Solve the Problem

3 Use this work space.

4 _____ apples were left.

Check Your Work

5 Do your answers make sense?   ○ yes   ○ no

**CCMS
1.OA.C.6** Use equivalent or known sums to add or subtract.

Math Fundamentals • EMC 3081 • © Evan-Moor Corp.

Equivalency and Unknown Numbers

Domain

Operations and Algebraic Thinking

Cluster

Work with addition and subtraction equations.

Standards in Cluster

1.OA.D.7 Understand the meaning of the equal sign, and determine if equations involving addition and subtraction are true or false. For example, which of the following equations are true and which are false? $6 = 6$; $7 = 8 - 1$; $5 + 2 = 2 + 5$; $4 + 1 = 5 + 2$.

1.OA.D.8 Determine the unknown whole number in an addition or subtraction equation relating three whole numbers. For example, determine the unknown number that makes the equation true in each of the equations $8 + ? = 11$; $5 = \_ - 3$; $6 + 6 = \_$.

Unit Contents

Mathematical Practices in This Unit

Make sense of problems and persevere in solving them: *pages 77, 82*

Reason abstractly and quantitatively: *pages 74, 75, 76, 77, 78, 79, 80, 81, 82*

Construct viable arguments and critique the reasoning of others: *pages 74, 78*

Model with mathematics: *pages 77, 82*

Attend to precision: *pages 74, 77, 78, 82*

Look for and make use of structure: *pages 74, 75, 76, 77, 78, 79, 80, 81, 82*

Math Models

Determining equivalency

You can find out if addition or subtraction number sentences are true or false.

Numbers on both sides of = should have the same value.

These are some examples:

True 😊	False 🙁
$3 = 3$	$3 = 4$
$6 = 7 - 1$ $6 = 6$	$6 = 7 + 1$ $6 = 8$
$5 + 3 = 4 + 4$ $8 = 8$	$5 + 3 = 4 + 6$ $8 = 10$

Think

Is **7 + 2 = 6 + 3** true or false? Explain your thinking.

 CCMS 1.OA.D.7 Understand the meaning of the equal sign. Determine if addition or subtraction equations are true or false.

Math Fundamentals • EMC 3081 • © Evan-Moor Corp.

Look at each number sentence.

Circle true or false .

Example

$12 = 6 + 7$

$12 = 13$

true

false

❶ $15 = 15$

true

false

❷ $5 + 8 = 4 + 10$

true

false

❸ $18 - 9 = 6 + 3$

true

false

Understand the meaning of the equal sign.
Determine if addition or subtraction equations are true or false.

CCMS
1.0A.D.7

75

Look at each number sentence.
Circle true 😊 or false 🙁.

---

1 $16 = 61$

true

false

---

2 $2 + 11 = 11 + 2$

true

false

---

3 $5 + 2 = 17 - 10$

true

false

---

4 $8 + 6 = 7 + 7$

true

false

CCMS 1.OA.D.7 Understand the meaning of the equal sign.
Determine if addition or subtraction equations are true or false.

Name _____

Read the Problem

Pat has 3 pink shirts and 4 white shirts.
Fran has 5 pink shirts and 2 white shirts.
Do Pat and Fran have the same number of shirts?

Think About It

1 You will find out if Pat and Fran have _____.

  ○ more pink than white shirts   ○ the same number of shirts

2 Mark the number sentence that tells about the problem.

  ○ $3 + 4 = 5 - 2$ ○ $3 + 4 = 5 + 2$ ○ $4 - 3 = 5 - 2$

Solve the Problem

3 Use this work space.

4 Pat and Fran have the same number of shirts.

  ○ yes   ○ no

Check Your Work

5 Do your answers make sense?   ○ yes   ○ no

Understand the meaning of the equal sign.
Determine if addition or subtraction equations are true or false.

You can find the unknown number to make a number sentence that is true.

$$? + 4 = 7$$

Both sides of **=** need the same value.

These are some ways to find an unknown number to make a true number sentence:

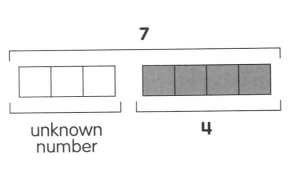

You can take apart the sum.

7

unknown number

4

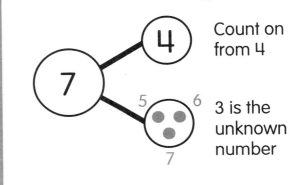

You can use a diagram.

7

4

Count on from 4

5 6
7

3 is the unknown number

$$3 + 4 = 7$$

$$7 = 7 \text{ is true. } ☺$$

Think

Think of **11 + 9 = ?** Which is true: **11 + 9 = 19** or **11 + 9 = 20**? Explain your thinking.

CCMS 1.OA.D.8 Determine the unknown whole number to make a true equation.

Math Fundamentals • EMC 3081 • © Evan-Moor Corp.

Mark the number that makes each number sentence true.
Show your work.

Example

6 + __?__ = 14

● 8   ○ 9

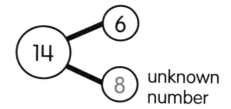

unknown
number

Work Space

❶ __?__ + 7 = 11

○ 3   ○ 4

❷ 8 + 9 = __?__

○ 17   ○ 18

❸ 10 = 15 – __?__

○ 4   ○ 5

Determine the unknown whole number to make a true equation.   **CCMS 1.OA.D.8**

Mark the number that makes each number sentence true.
Show your work.

Work Space

1 $3 + \underline{} = 15$

○ 11   ○ 12

2 $19 = \underline{} + 8$

○ 10   ○ 11

3 $\underline{} + 7 = 12$

○ 5   ○ 6

4 $6 + 5 = \underline{}$

○ 10   ○ 11

CCMS
1.OA.D.8 Determine the unknown whole number to make a true equation.

Write the unknown number that makes each number sentence true.
Mark the model that tells about the number sentence.

Example

$6 + \underline{4} = 10$

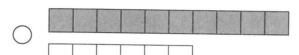

1 $\underline{} + 11 = 16$

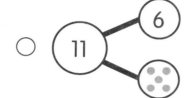

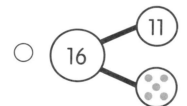

2 $15 - 9 = \underline{}$

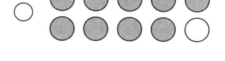

3 $20 = \underline{} + 8$

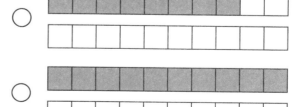

Name _____

Read the Problem

Travis had 12 rocks in his pocket. Some rocks fell out.
Travis had 7 rocks left. How many rocks fell out?

Think About It

1 You will find out how many rocks _____.

○ fell out   ○ Travis had   ○ in all

2 Mark **two** number sentences that are true.

○ $12 = 7 + 5$ ○ $12 + 5 = 16$ ○ $12 - 5 = 7$

Solve the Problem

3 Use this work space.

4 _____ rocks fell out.

Check Your Work

5 Do your answers make sense?   ○ yes   ○ no

CCMS
1.OA.D.8 Determine the unknown whole number to make a true equation.

Math Fundamentals • EMC 3081 • © Evan-Moor Corp.

Counting and Number Sequences

Domain

Number and Operations in Base Ten

Cluster

Extend the counting sequence.

Standard in Cluster

1.NBT.A.1 Count to 120, starting at any number less than 120. In this range, read and write numerals and represent a number of objects with a written numeral.

Unit Contents

Mathematical Practices in This Unit

Make sense of problems and persevere in solving them: *pages 88, 92, 96, 100, 104*

Reason abstractly and quantitatively: *pages 84, 85, 86, 87, 88, 89, 90, 91, 92, 93, 94, 95, 96, 97, 98, 99, 100, 101, 102, 103, 104*

Construct viable arguments and critique the reasoning of others: *pages 84, 89, 93, 97, 101*

Model with mathematics: *pages 84, 85, 86, 87, 88, 89, 90, 91, 92, 93, 94, 95, 96, 97, 98, 99, 100, 101, 102, 103, 104*

Attend to precision: *pages 84, 85, 86, 87, 88, 89, 90, 91, 92, 93, 94, 95, 96, 97, 98, 99, 100, 101, 102, 103, 104*

Look for and make use of structure: *pages 84, 85, 86, 87, 88, 89, 90, 91, 92, 93, 94, 95, 96, 97, 98, 99, 100, 101, 102, 103, 104*

Look for and express regularity in repeated reasoning: *pages 84, 85, 86, 87, 89, 90, 91, 92, 93, 94, 95, 96, 97, 98, 99, 100, 101, 102, 103, 104*

Math Models
Counting from zero

You can count to tell how many.

These are some ways you can count things that are real:

You can draw a picture.	You can use a chart.
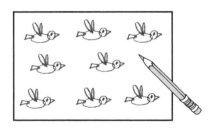	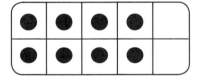

You can use a number line.

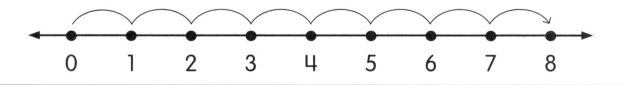

Think

Ben says it is easier to draw ● than 🐦 to show **8**.
Do you agree? Explain your thinking.

CCMS 1.NBT.A.1 Count objects.
Read and write numerals that represent a number of objects.

Math Fundamentals • EMC 3081 • © Evan-Moor Corp.

Show some ways to count things.

Examples

Count to 13.

Draw a picture. | Draw a chart. | Draw a number line.

 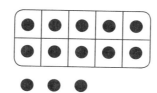 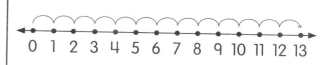

Count to 20.

1 Draw a picture.

2 Draw a chart.

3 Draw a number line.

Count objects.
Read and write numerals that represent a number of objects.

CCMS
1.NBT.A.1

85

Name _____

Count how many. Write the number.

1 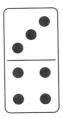 _____ dots

2  _____ butterflies

3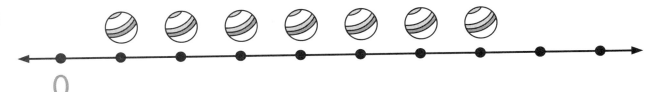

0 ___ ___ ___ ___ ___ ___ ___

_____ balls

4  _____ hearts

5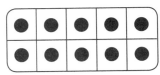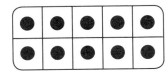

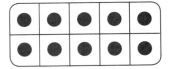 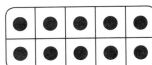 _____ dots

CCMS 1.NBT.A.1 Count objects. Read and write numerals that represent a number of objects.

Math Fundamentals • EMC 3081 • © Evan-Moor Corp.

Look at the picture next to each item. Count how many in the picture above. Color or mark each item you count. Write the number on the line.

1  _____

2 _____

3  _____

4 _____

5 _____

6 _____

Count objects.
Read and write numerals that represent a number of objects.

Name _____

Read the Problem

Count the chairs in your classroom.
Draw a model in the work space below.
Write the number that tells how many.

Think About It

1 The problem says to _____.
  ○ sit on the chairs   ○ count the chairs

2 What kind of model will you draw?
  ○ picture   ○ chart   ○ number line   ○ other

Solve the Problem

3 Use this work space.

4 There are _____ chairs.

Check Your Work

5 Do your answers make sense?   ○ yes   ○ no

You can count on from any number.

You know that 20 cars are in the box. You can count on from 20 to find out how many cars there are.

21 22 23

These are some ways to **count on**:

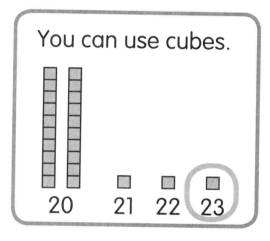

You can use cubes.

20   21   22   23

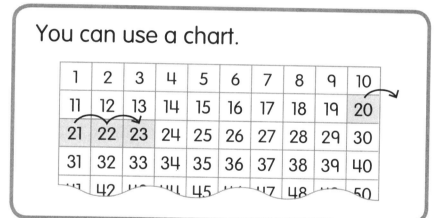

You can use a chart.

1	2	3	4	5	6	7	8	9	10
11	12	13	14	15	16	17	18	19	20
21	22	23	24	25	26	27	28	29	30
31	32	33	34	35	36	37	38	39	40
41	42	43	44	45	46	47	48	49	50

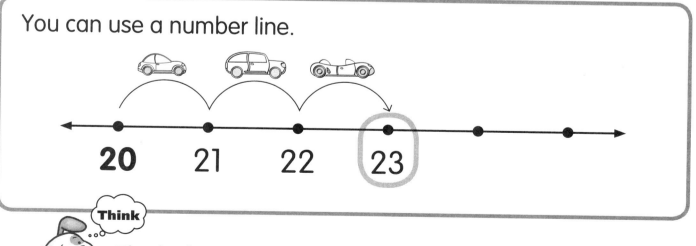

You can use a number line.

20   21   22   23

Think

Think about a time you can use **counting on**.

Count, starting with any number.
Represent a number of objects with a numeral.

CCMS
1.NBT.A.1

Name _____

Count on to tell how many. Write the numbers.

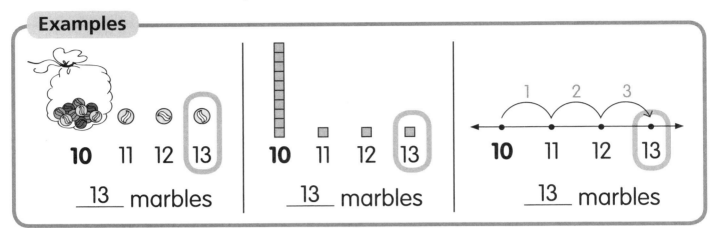

Examples

10 11 12 13   ___13___ marbles

10 11 12 13   ___13___ marbles

1 2 3
10 11 12 13   ___13___ marbles

1

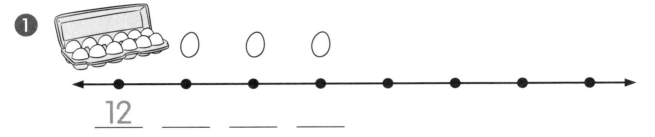

12 ___ ___ ___

_____ eggs

2

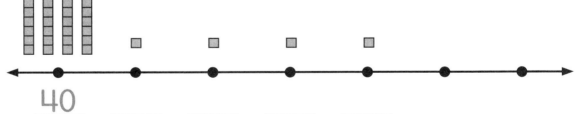

40 ___ ___ ___ ___

_____ cubes

3

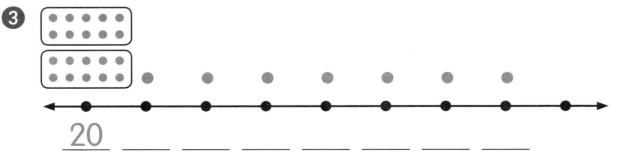

20 ___ ___ ___ ___ ___ ___ ___

_____ dots

CCMS
1.NBT.A.1 Count, starting with any number.
Represent a number of objects with a numeral.

Math Fundamentals • EMC 3081 • © Evan-Moor Corp.

Count on to tell how many. Write the numbers.

1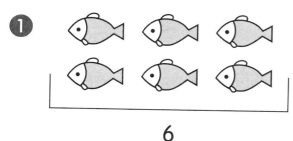

6   ____ ____   ____ fish

2

10   ____ ____ ____ ____ ____ cups

3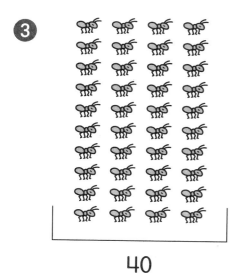

40   ____ ____ ____ ____ ____ ants

Count, starting with any number.
Represent a number of objects with a numeral.

CCMS
1.NBT.A.1

Name _____

Read the Problem

A frog needs help finding its pond. Count on from 4.
Write the missing numbers from 1 to 50.

Think About It

1 The problem says to _____.
○ count on from 1   ○ count on from 4

2 You will write the missing numbers.   ○ yes   ○ no

Solve the Problem

3

Check Your Work

4 Do your answers make sense?   ○ yes   ○ no

CCMS
1.NBT.A.1
Count, starting with any number.
Represent a number of objects with a numeral.

Math Fundamentals • EMC 3081 • © Evan-Moor Corp.

You can count on from a large number.

You know there are 60 apples. You can count on from 60 to find out how many apples there are.

60   61   62   63   64

These are some ways to **count on**:

You can use cubes.

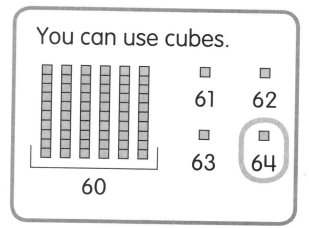

61   62
63   64
60

You can use a chart.

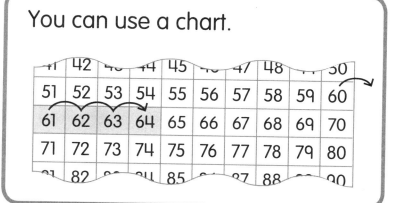

41	42	43	44	45	46	47	48	49	50
51	52	53	54	55	56	57	58	59	60
61	62	63	64	65	66	67	68	69	70
71	72	73	74	75	76	77	78	79	80
81	82	83	84	85	86	87	88	89	90

You can use a number line.

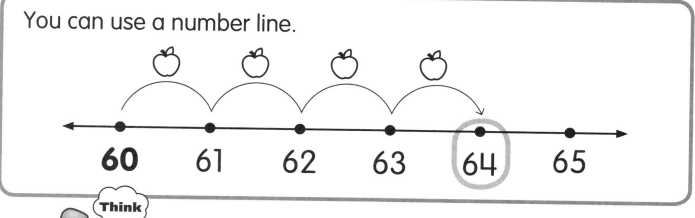

60   61   62   63   64   65

Think

Explain how you can count on 🍎🍎🍎🍎 from **99** apples.

Count to 120, starting at any number.
Represent a number of objects with a numeral.

CCMS 1.NBT.A.1   **93**

Count on from each number. Write the numbers.

Examples

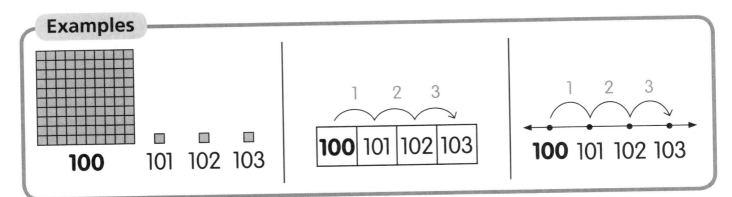

1

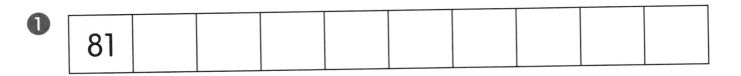

81									

2

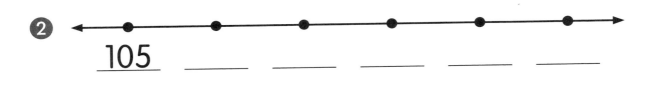

105 ___ ___ ___ ___ ___

3

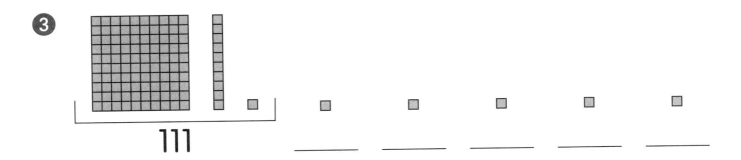

111 ___ ___ ___ ___ ___

CCMS
1.NBT.A.1 Count to 120, starting at any number.
Represent a number of objects with a numeral.

Math Fundamentals • EMC 3081 • © Evan-Moor Corp.

Count on from each number. Write the numbers.

1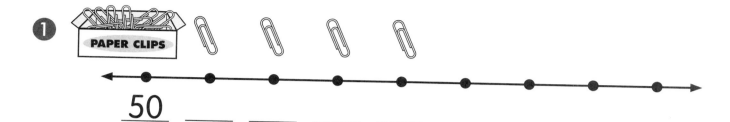

50 ___ ___ ___ ___

___ paper clips

2

74						

3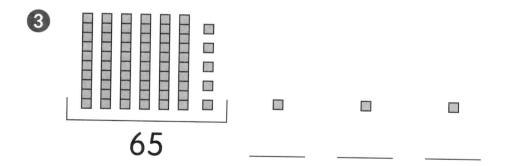

65 ___ ___ ___

4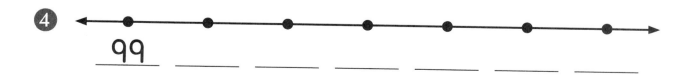

99 ___ ___ ___ ___ ___ ___ ___

Count to 120, starting at any number.
Represent a number of objects with a numeral.

CCMS
1.NBT.A.1   95

Read the Problem

A bird needs help finding the way to its nest.
Color the boxes that count in order from 90 to 120.

Think About It

1 I need to find numbers that _____.
   ○ count from 90 to 120   ○ count from 19 to 100

Solve the Problem

2

90	91	92	93	60	43	29	74	52	80
44	19	40	94	95	96	97	98	99	61
30	98	36	79	63	68	51	43	100	39
109	108	107	106	105	104	103	102	101	37
110	77	64	65	54	42	84	50	25	79
111	112	113	114	115	116	117	118	119	120

Check Your Work

3 Do your answers make sense?   ○ yes   ○ no

CCMS 1.NBT.A.1 Count to 120, starting at any number.
Represent a number of objects with a numeral.

Math Fundamentals • EMC 3081 • © Evan-Moor Corp.

You can skip count groups of things.

You can skip count by **tens**.

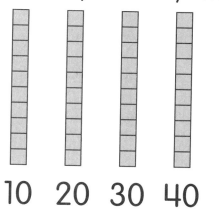

10 20 30 40

You can skip count by **fives**.

5   10   15   20

You can skip count by **twos**.

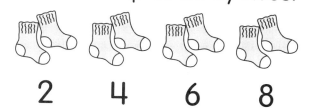

2   4   6   8

These are some ways to **skip count**:

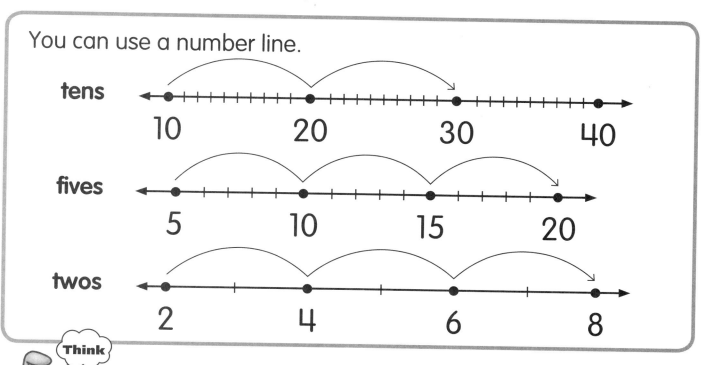

You can use a number line.

tens

10   20   30   40

fives

5   10   15   20

twos

2   4   6   8

Think

Skip count by tens, fives, and twos up to **100**.
You can use a **100** chart.

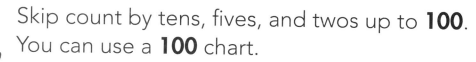

© Evan-Moor Corp. • EMC 3081 • Math Fundamentals

Count, starting at any number.
Represent a number of objects with a numeral.

**CCMS
1.NBT.A.1**

97

Skip count by tens, fives, or twos. Write the missing numbers.

Examples

I see groups of two eyes. I can count by twos.

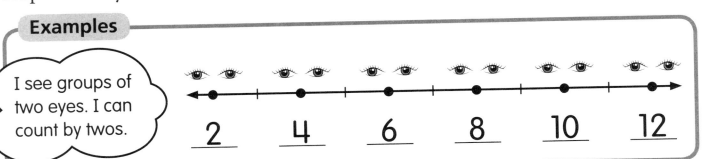

2   4   6   8   10   12

1

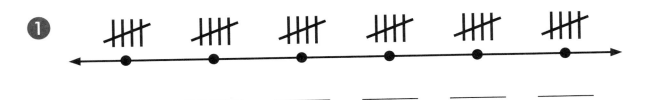

___ ___ ___ ___ ___ ___

2

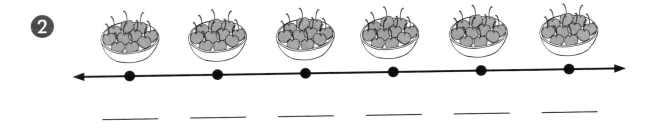

___ ___ ___ ___ ___ ___

3

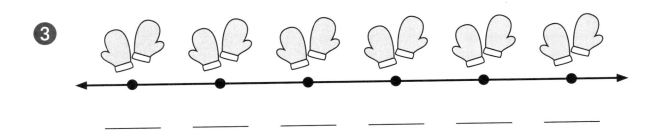

___ ___ ___ ___ ___ ___

CCMS
1.NBT.A.1 Count, starting at any number.
Represent a number of objects with a numeral.

Math Fundamentals • EMC 3081 • © Evan-Moor Corp.

Name _____

Skip count.

❶ Count by tens. Color each number you counted **yellow**.
❷ Count by fives. Draw a circle around each number you counted.
❸ Count by twos. Draw an **X** on each number you counted.

1	2	3	4	5	6	7	8	9	10
11	12	13	14	15	16	17	18	19	20
21	22	23	24	25	26	27	28	29	30
31	32	33	34	35	36	37	38	39	40
41	42	43	44	45	46	47	48	49	50
51	52	53	54	55	56	57	58	59	60
61	62	63	64	65	66	67	68	69	70
71	72	73	74	75	76	77	78	79	80
81	82	83	84	85	86	87	88	89	90
91	92	93	94	95	96	97	98	99	100
101	102	103	104	105	106	107	108	109	110
111	112	113	114	115	116	117	118	119	120

Count, starting at any number.
Represent a number of objects with a numeral.

CCMS 1.NBT.A.1 · 99

Name _____

Read the Problem

Dan counted how many people were at the beach.
He counted ||||| ||||| ||||| ||||| ||||| ||||| people.
Write the number in the work space.

Think About It

1 Dan _____ the people.
  ○ played with   ○ counted   ○ lost

2 You can count Dan's marks by _____.
  ○ fives   ○ twos

Solve the Problem

3 Use this work space.

4 There were _____ people at the beach.

Check Your Work

5 Do your answers make sense?   ○ yes   ○ no

CCMS
1.NBT.A.1 Count, starting at any number.
Represent a number of objects with a numeral.

Math Fundamentals • EMC 3081 • © Evan-Moor Corp.

You can count back from any number.

Sometimes you need to count back.

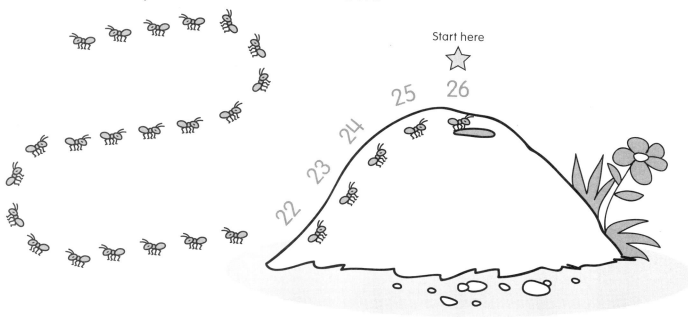

These are some ways to **count back**:

You can use a number line.

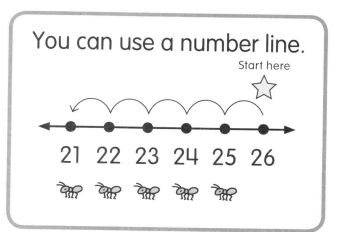

You can use a chart.

1	2	3	4	5	6	7	8	9	10
11	12	13	14	15	16	17	18	19	20
21	22	23	24	25	26	27	28	29	30
31	32	33	34	35	36	37	38	39	40
41	42	43	44	45	46	47	48	49	50

Think

Try counting back from **50** to **1** without looking at a chart or a number line.

Read and write numerals that represent a number of objects.

Name _____

Count back. Write the missing numbers.

Examples

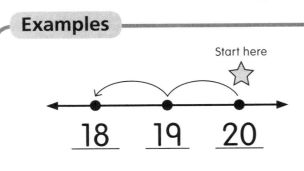
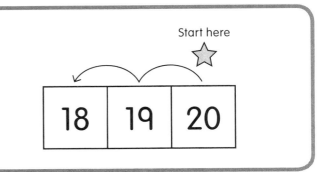

1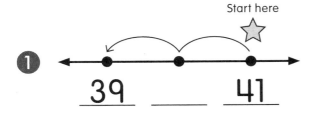

39 ____ 41

2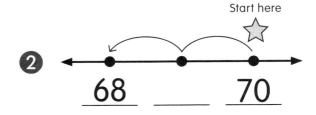

68 ____ 70

3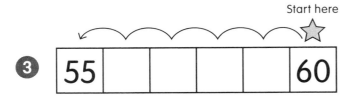

4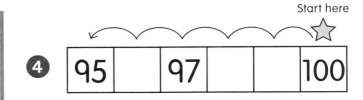

5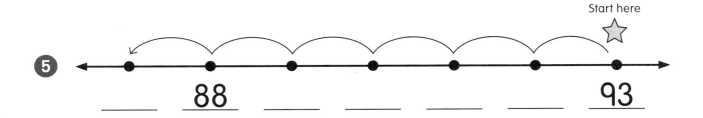

____ 88 ____ ____ ____ ____ 93

6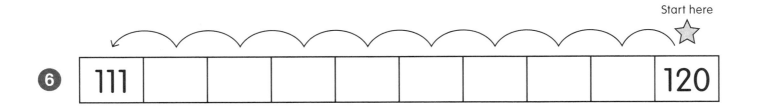

CCMS
1.NBT.A.1 Read and write numerals that represent a number of objects.

Math Fundamentals • EMC 3081 • © Evan-Moor Corp.

Count back. Write the missing numbers.

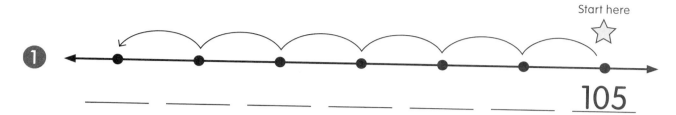

1 105

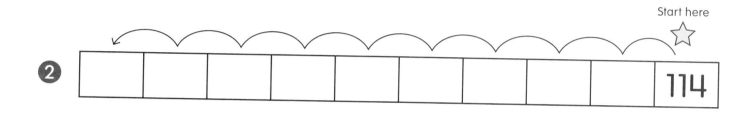

2 114

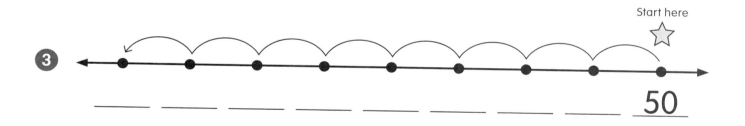

3 50

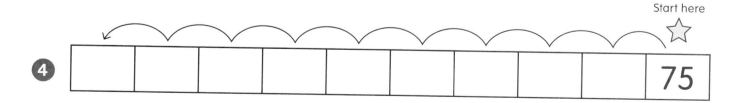

4 75

Read and write numerals that represent a number of objects.

**CCMS
1.NBT.A.1** 103

Name _____

Read the Problem

Mrs. Beck said to count back from 103 to 98.
Finish the number line.
Write the numbers.

Think About It

1 You will _____.
○ skip count   ○ count on   ○ count back

2 You will write numbers on a _____.
○ number line   ○ chart

Solve the Problem

3 Use this work space.

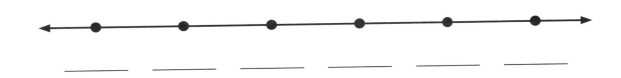

Check Your Work

4 Do your answers make sense?   ○ yes   ○ no

CCMS 1.NBT.A.1 Read and write numerals that represent a number of objects.

Math Fundamentals • EMC 3081 • © Evan-Moor Corp.

Place Value: Two-Digit Numbers

Domain

Number and Operations in Base Ten

Cluster

Understand place value: Two-digit numbers.

Standards in Cluster

1.NBT.B.2 Understand that the two digits of a two-digit number represent amounts of tens and ones. Understand the following as special cases:

1.NBT.B.2.a 10 can be thought of as a bundle of ten ones—called a "ten."

1.NBT.B.2.b The numbers from 11 to 19 are composed of a ten and one, two, three, four, five, six, seven, eight, or nine ones.

1.NBT.B.2.c The numbers 10, 20, 30, 40, 50, 60, 70, 80, 90 refer to one, two, three, four, five, six, seven, eight, or nine tens (and 0 ones).

1.NBT.B.3 Compare two two-digit numbers based on meanings of the tens and ones digits, recording the results of comparisons with the symbols >, =, and <.

Unit Contents

Mathematical Practices in This Unit

Make sense of problems and persevere in solving them: *pages 109, 113, 118*

Reason abstractly and quantitatively: *pages 106, 107, 108, 109, 110, 111, 112, 113, 114, 115, 116, 117, 118*

Construct viable arguments and critique the reasoning of others: *pages 106, 109, 110, 114*

Model with mathematics: *pages 106, 107, 108, 109, 110, 111, 112, 113, 114, 115, 116, 117, 118*

Attend to precision: *pages 106, 109, 110, 113, 114, 118*

Look for and make use of structure: *pages 106, 107, 108, 110, 111, 112, 114, 115, 116, 117*

Look for and express regularity in repeated reasoning: *pages 106, 107, 108, 111, 112, 114, 116, 117*

You can tell how many groups of ten are in a two-digit number.

These are two examples:

Number	Model	Tens	Ones
10 tens ones		1	0
20 tens ones		2	0

Think

How many tens are in the numbers **30**, **50**, and **80**? Explain your thinking.

1.NBT.B.2
1.NBT.B.2.a
1.NBT.B.2.c
Understand two-digit numbers as tens and ones.

Math Fundamentals • EMC 3081 • © Evan-Moor Corp.

Look at each number. Draw a line to the tens for each number.

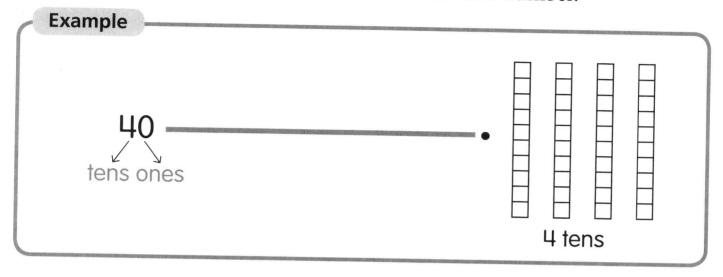

Example

40
tens ones

4 tens

1 20

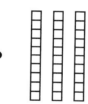

2 80

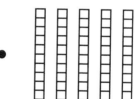

3 30

4 50

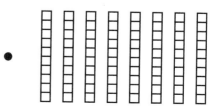

Look at each group of cubes. Write the number that tells how many.

1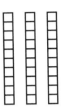

_30_

4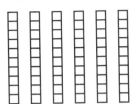

_____

2

_____

5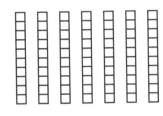

_____

3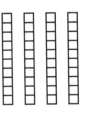

_____

6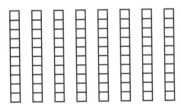

_____

1.NBT.B.2
1.NBT.B.2.a Understand two-digit numbers as tens and ones.
1.NBT.B.2.c

Name _____

Read the Problem

Mrs. Beck has 3 boxes of pencils.
Each box has 10 pencils.
Tyson says Mrs. Beck has 30 pencils.
Do you agree?

Think About It

1 You will find out if Mrs. Beck has _____.

○ 3 boxes   ○ 10 pencils   ○ 30 pencils

2 How many tens are in **30**?

○ 30 tens   ○ 3 tens   ○ 0 tens

Solve the Problem

3 Use this work space.

4 Mrs. Beck has 30 pencils.   ○ yes   ○ no

Check Your Work

5 Do your answers make sense?   ○ yes   ○ no

You can show how two-digit numbers are made up of tens and ones.

These are some examples:

Number	Model	Tens	Ones
11 tens ones		1	1
22 tens ones		2	2
45 tens ones		4	5

Think

For each number **13** through **19**, tell the number of tens and ones. Do you notice a pattern? Explain your thinking.

110 CCMS 1.NBT.B.2 1.NBT.B.2.b Understand two-digit numbers as tens and ones.

Math Fundamentals • EMC 3081 • © Evan-Moor Corp.

Draw a model. Then write how many tens and ones.

Example

Number	Model	Tens	Ones
25 tens ones		2	5

Number	Model	Tens	Ones
1 16			
2 31			
3 52			

Understand two-digit numbers as tens and ones.

Mark the value of each underlined digit.

1

1<u>9</u>
○ 9 ones
○ 9 tens

5

<u>3</u>0
○ 3 ones
○ 3 tens

2

<u>5</u>8
○ 5 ones
○ 5 tens

6

6<u>2</u>
○ 2 ones
○ 2 tens

3

9<u>0</u>
○ 0 ones
○ 9 tens

7

7<u>5</u>
○ 5 ones
○ 7 tens

4

<u>8</u>3
○ 3 ones
○ 8 tens

8

<u>4</u>9
○ 9 ones
○ 4 tens

CCMS 1.NBT.B.2 1.NBT.B.2.b Understand two-digit numbers as tens and ones.

Math Fundamentals • EMC 3081 • © Evan-Moor Corp.

Read the Problem

Mr. Lau said, "Guess my number!
It has 5 tens and 9 ones.
What number is it?"

Think About It

1 You will find out what number _____.

○ has 5 tens and 9 ones   ○ has 5 ones and 9 tens

2 Mr. Lau's number has _____.

○ one digit   ○ two digits   ○ three digits

Solve the Problem

3 Use this work space.

4 The number is _____.

Check Your Work

5 Do your answers make sense?   ○ yes   ○ no

Understand two-digit numbers as tens and ones.

You can use $>$, $=$, and $<$ to compare two-digit numbers.

These are some examples:

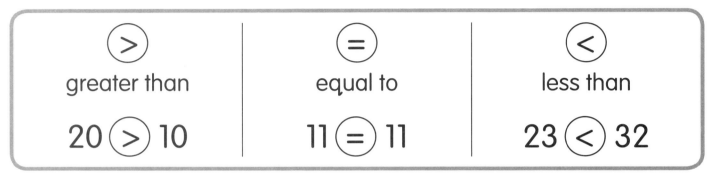

$>$ greater than	$=$ equal to	$<$ less than
$20 > 10$	$11 = 11$	$23 < 32$

Steps to compare **two-digit numbers**:

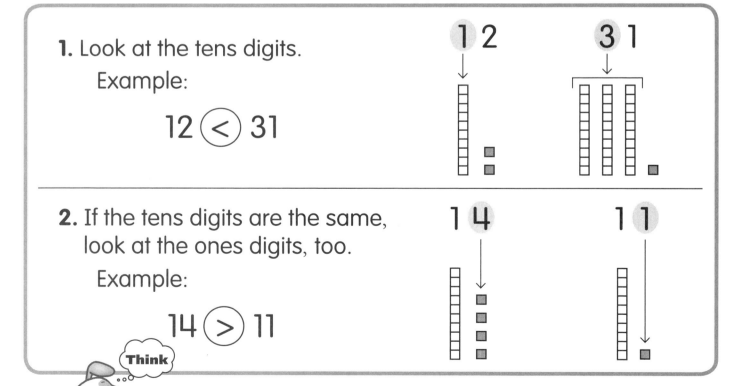

1. Look at the tens digits.
Example:

$12 < 31$

2. If the tens digits are the same, look at the ones digits, too.
Example:

$14 > 11$

Think

Is **72 < 27** true? Explain your thinking.

CCMS 1.NBT.B.3 Compare two two-digit numbers based on meanings of the tens and ones digits.

Math Fundamentals • EMC 3081 • © Evan-Moor Corp.

Name _____

Write **>**, **=**, or **<** to make a true number sentence. Then draw a model.

Examples

23 $<$ 32

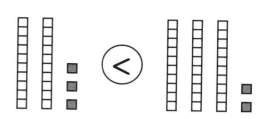

1 15 $\bigcirc$ 15

2 27 $\bigcirc$ 32

3 31 $\bigcirc$ 21

Compare two two-digit numbers based on meanings
of the tens and ones digits.

CCMS
1.NBT.B.3 115

Write **>**, **=**, or **<** to make a true number sentence. Then draw a model.

1

_____

2

_____

3 40 ◯ 39

_____

4 52 ◯ 52

116 **CCMS 1.NBT.B.3** Compare two two-digit numbers based on meanings of the tens and ones digits.

Math Fundamentals • EMC 3081 • © Evan-Moor Corp.

Write a **two-digit** number to complete each number sentence.
Then draw a model.

1 ____ = 12

4 ____ > 12

2 43 > ____

5 43 < ____

3 50 = ____

6 ____ < 50

Compare two two-digit numbers based on meanings
of the tens and ones digits.

Name _____

Read the Problem

Chris read 59 books. Dan read 61 books.

Use **>**, **=**, or **<**.

Write a number sentence to compare **59** and **61**.

Think About It

1 You will write a _____.

○ word problem   ○ number sentence   ○ math book

2 Mark the symbol that you can **not** use.

○ **>** greater than   ○ **=** equal to   ○ **<** less than

Solve the Problem

3 Use this work space.

4 Number sentence: _____ ◯ _____

Check Your Work

5 Do your answers make sense?   ○ yes   ○ no

CCMS 1.NBT.B.3 Compare two two-digit numbers based on meanings of the tens and ones digits.

Math Fundamentals • EMC 3081 • © Evan-Moor Corp.

Place Value: Addition and Subtraction

Domain

Number and Operations in Base Ten

Cluster

Use place value understanding and properties of operations to add and subtract.

Standards in Cluster

1.NBT.C.4 Add within 100, including adding a two-digit number and a one-digit number, and adding a two-digit number and a multiple of 10, using concrete models or drawings and strategies based on place value, properties of operations, and/or the relationship between addition and subtraction; relate the strategy to a written method and explain the reasoning used. Understand that in adding two-digit numbers, one adds tens and tens, ones and ones; and sometimes it is necessary to compose a ten.

1.NBT.C.5 Given a two-digit number, mentally find 10 more or 10 less than the number, without having to count; explain the reasoning used.

1.NBT.C.6 Subtract multiples of 10 in the range 10–90 from multiples of 10 in the range 10–90 (positive or zero differences), using concrete models or drawings and strategies based on place value, properties of operations, and/or the relationship between addition and subtraction; relate the strategy to a written method and explain the reasoning used.

Unit Contents

Mathematical Practices in This Unit

Make sense of problems and persevere in solving them: *pages 123, 127, 131, 132*

Reason abstractly and quantitatively: *pages 120, 121, 122, 123, 124, 125, 126, 127, 128, 129, 130, 131*

Construct viable arguments and critique the reasoning of others: *pages 120, 124, 128*

Model with mathematics: *pages 120, 121, 122, 123, 124, 125, 126, 127, 128, 129, 130, 131*

Attend to precision: *pages 120, 121, 122, 123, 124, 125, 126, 127, 128, 129, 130, 131*

Look for and make use of structure: *pages 120, 121, 122, 124, 125, 126, 128, 129, 130, 131*

Math Models

Adding two-digit numbers within 100

Sometimes you need to compose a ten when you add two-digit numbers.

Add tens and tens.
Add ones and ones.

These are some examples:

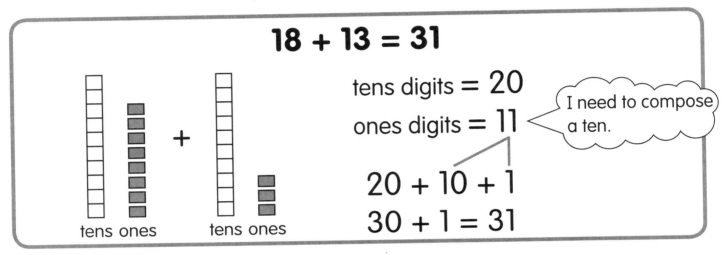

$$18 + 13 = 31$$

tens digits = 20
ones digits = 11

I need to compose a ten.

20 + 10 + 1
30 + 1 = 31

tens ones   tens ones

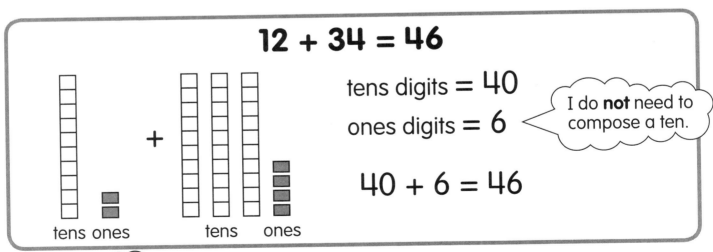

$$12 + 34 = 46$$

tens digits = 40
ones digits = 6

I do **not** need to compose a ten.

40 + 6 = 46

tens ones   tens   ones

Think

Explain how you can solve **48 + 9** and **32 + 10**.

CCMS 1.NBT.C.4 In adding two-digit numbers, it is sometimes necessary to compose a ten.

Math Fundamentals • EMC 3081 • © Evan-Moor Corp.

Name _____

Add. Compose a ten if you need to.

Example

$40 + 13$ — I need to compose a ten.

$36 + 17 = \underline{53}$

$40 + 10 + 3$

$50 + 3 = 53$

Work Space

1

$42 + 20 = \underline{\hspace{1cm}}$

2

$61 + 17 = \underline{\hspace{1cm}}$

3

$57 + 15 = \underline{\hspace{1cm}}$

Add. Compose a ten if you need to.

Work Space

 1

$$60 + 27 = \underline{\hspace{1cm}}$$

 2

$$28 + 36 = \underline{\hspace{1cm}}$$

3

$$91 + 6 = \underline{\hspace{1cm}}$$

4

$$59 + 23 = \underline{\hspace{1cm}}$$

**CCMS
1.NBT.C.4** In adding two-digit numbers, it is sometimes necessary to compose a ten.

Math Fundamentals • EMC 3081 • © Evan-Moor Corp.

Read the Problem

26 girls and 25 boys rode on the bus.
How many children rode on the bus altogether?

Think About It

1 You will find out how many children _____.

○ were girls   ○ got off the bus   ○ rode on the bus

2 Will you need to compose a ten?

○ yes   ○ no

Solve the Problem

3 Use this work space.

4 _____ children rode on the bus altogether.

Check Your Work

5 Do your answers make sense?   ○ yes   ○ no

© Evan-Moor Corp. • EMC 3081 • Math Fundamentals

In adding two-digit numbers, it is sometimes necessary to compose a ten.

CCMS
1.NBT.C.4 **123**

You can find ten more or ten less than a number without counting.

Let's find 10 more and 10 less than **15**.

One way is to think of a number chart.

Ten **less** than 15

Ten **more** than 15

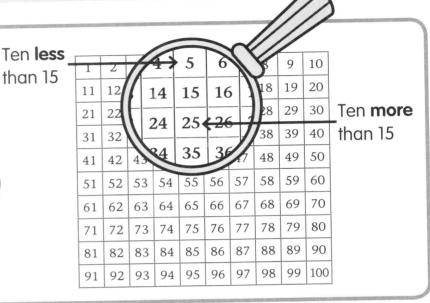

Another way is to think of skipping back or forward by ten from any number.

Ten less
12

22

Ten more
32

Skip **back** by ten

Skip **forward** by ten

Think

Try mental math. What number is **ten more** than **89**? What number is **ten less** than **89**? Explain your thinking.

CCMS 1.NBT.C.5 Given a two-digit number, mentally find 10 more or 10 less than the number.

Look at each number. Write ten more or ten less.

Examples

Ten More	Ten Less
27	13
37	23

Ten More

Ten Less

❶
60

❷
31

❺
19

❻
24

❸
76

❹
58

❼
47

❽
82

Given a two-digit number, mentally find 10 more or 10 less than the number.

Look at each number. Write ten more or ten less.

Ten More

1 11 _____

3 63 _____

2 27 _____

4 75 _____

Ten Less

5 _____ 12

7 _____ 36

6 _____ 53

8 _____ 99

CCMS 1.NBT.C.5   Given a two-digit number, mentally find 10 more or 10 less than the number.

Math Fundamentals • EMC 3081 • © Evan-Moor Corp.

Name _____

Read the Problem

I planted 25 seeds in the garden.
Mom planted 10 more seeds than I did.
How many seeds did Mom plant?

Think About It

1 You will find out how many seeds _____.
○ Mom planted   ○ I planted

2 Mark the number sentence that tells about the problem.
○ 25 − 10 = ?   ○ ? + 10 = 25   ○ 25 + 10 = ?

Solve the Problem

3 Use this work space.

4 Mom planted _____ seeds.

Check Your Work

5 Do your answers make sense?   ○ yes   ○ no

You can subtract a multiple of ten from another multiple of ten.

These are some multiples of ten:

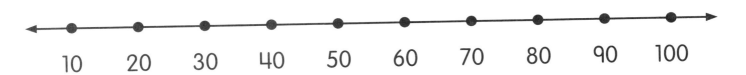

10   20   30   40   50   60   70   80   90   100

Let's subtract $50 - 20 = ?$

These are two ways to show it:

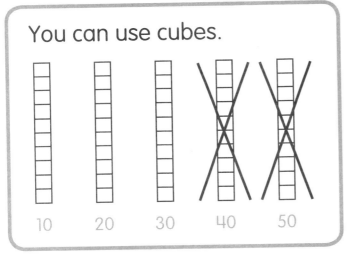

You can use cubes.

10   20   30   40   50

$$50 - 20 = 30$$
↑   ↑   ↑

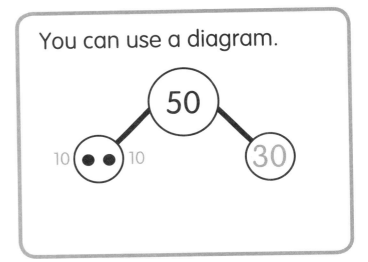

You can use a diagram.

50

10   10

30

$$50 - 20 = 30$$
↑   ↑   ↑

Think

Choose a way to solve **70 – 30 = ?** Explain your thinking.

128   **CCMS 1.NBT.C.6**   Subtract multiples of ten from multiples of ten.
Show a model or strategy and explain the reasoning.

Math Fundamentals • EMC 3081 • © Evan-Moor Corp.

Subtract. Show your work.

Example

70 – 30 = __40__

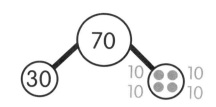

Work Space

 1

50 – 40 = ___

2

60 – 20 = ___

3

90 – 80 = ___

Subtract multiples of ten from multiples of ten.
Show a model or strategy and explain the reasoning.

CCMS
1.NBT.C.6   **129**

Complete each number sentence. Show your work.

Work Space

1

$80 - \underline{\quad} = 60$

2

$\underline{\quad} - 10 = 30$

3

$30 = 90 - \underline{\quad}$

4

$70 - \underline{\quad} = 20$

CCMS
1.NBT.C.6 Subtract multiples of ten from multiples of ten.
Show a model or strategy and explain the reasoning.

Math Fundamentals • EMC 3081 • © Evan-Moor Corp.

Draw a line from each number sentence to the model that can help you solve the problem. Write the answer.

1 90 – 70 = ____ •

•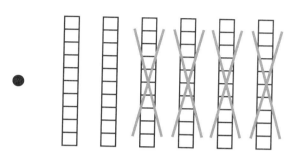

2 40 – ____ = 20 •

•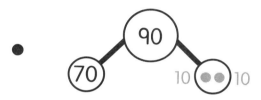

3 60 – 40 = ____ •

• 20 + 20 = 40

4 ____ – 10 = 40 •

•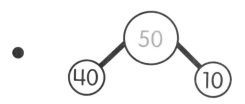

Subtract multiples of ten from multiples of ten.
Show a model or strategy and explain the reasoning.

Read the Problem

The store had 60 apples.
20 apples were sold.
How many apples were left?

Think About It

1 You will find out how many apples were _____.

○ sold   ○ left   ○ big

2 Mark the number sentence that tells about the problem.

○ ? = 60 − 20   ○ ? = 60 + 20   ○ ? = 80 − 20

Solve the Problem

3 Use this work space.

4 _____ apples were left.

Check Your Work

5 Do your answers make sense?   ○ yes   ○ no

CCMS
1.NBT.C.6
Subtract multiples of ten from multiples of ten.
Show a model or strategy and explain the reasoning.

Math Fundamentals • EMC 3081 • © Evan-Moor Corp.

Measuring Length

Domain

Measurement and Data

Cluster

Measure lengths indirectly and by iterating length units.

Standards in Cluster

1.MD.A.1 Order three objects by length; compare the lengths of two objects indirectly by using a third object.

1.MD.A.2 Express the length of an object as a whole number of length units, by laying multiple copies of a shorter object (the length unit) end to end; understand that the length measurement of an object is the number of same-size length units that span it with no gaps or overlaps. Limit to contexts where the object being measured is spanned by a whole number of length units with no gaps or overlaps.

Mathematical Practices in This Unit

Make sense of problems and persevere in solving them: *pages 137, 142*

Reason abstractly and quantitatively: *pages 134, 135, 136, 137, 138, 139, 140, 141, 142*

Construct viable arguments and critique the reasoning of others: *pages 134, 138*

Model with mathematics: *pages 135, 136, 137, 139, 140, 141, 142*

Attend to precision: *pages 134, 137, 138, 142*

Look for and make use of structure: *pages 134, 135, 136, 138, 139, 140, 141*

You can compare the length of objects and put them in order.

This is one way to compare and put things in order:

← This pencil is the **shortest**.

← This pencil is the **longest**.

This is another way to compare and put things in order:

This flower is the **tallest**.

This flower is the **shortest**.

Think

Why is it important to line up the pencils to compare their lengths? Explain your answer.

Follow the directions to number each group of things in order by length.

Example

Number the worms from **longest** to **shortest**.

_2_   _3_   _1_

❶ Number the dogs from **tallest** to **shortest**.

_____   _____   _____

❷ Number the bones from **shortest** to **longest**.

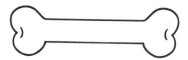 

_____   _____   _____

Follow the directions to number each group of things in order by length.

1 Number the crayons from **longest** to **shortest**.

_____   _____   _____

2 Number the sticks from **shortest** to **longest**.

_____   _____   _____

3 Number the trees from **tallest** to **shortest**.

_____   _____   _____

Name _____

Read the Problem

Mike has 3 leaves.
He wants to put them in order from **shortest** to **tallest**.
Mark the group that shows how he put the leaves in that order.

Think About It

1 You will mark three leaves that are in order from _____.

○ tallest to shortest   ○ shortest to tallest

2 The tallest leaf will be _____.

○ first   ○ in the middle   ○ last

Solve the Problem

3 Mark the group that is in order from **shortest** to **tallest**.

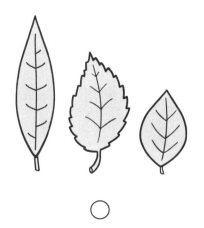   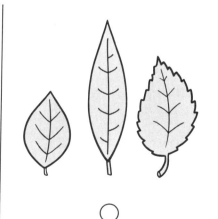   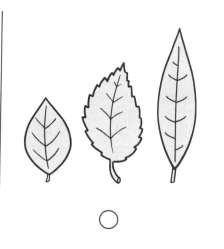

○   ○   ○

Check Your Work

4 Do your answers make sense?   ○ yes   ○ no

Math Models

Measuring and writing the length of objects

You can measure the length of objects.

One measuring tool you can use is cubes:

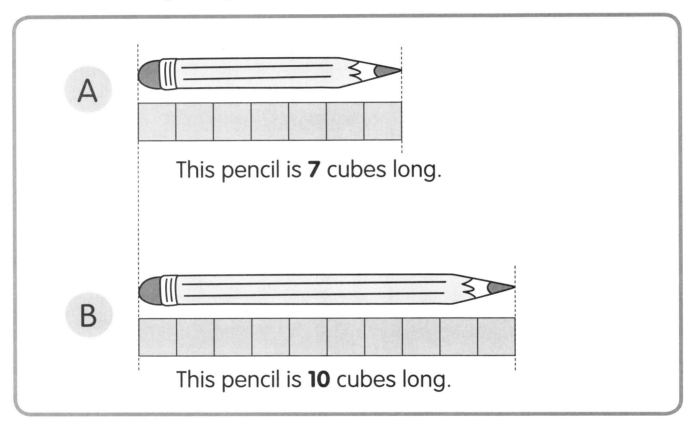

A

This pencil is **7** cubes long.

B

This pencil is **10** cubes long.

Pencil A is shorter than pencil B.
Pencil B is longer than pencil A.

Think

Explain what you can do if an object is lined up with the **second** cube.

CCMS
1.MD.A.1
1.MD.A.2
Compare the length of two objects by using a third object.
Use a short object to measure another object. Express the length as a whole number of length units.

Math Fundamentals • EMC 3081 • © Evan-Moor Corp.

Look at the paper clips to measure each item. Write the length.

Example

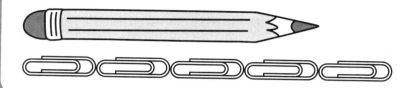

___4___ paper clips

1

_____ paper clips

2

_____ paper clips

3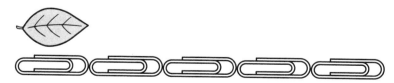

_____ paper clips

Compare the length of two objects by using a third object.
Use a short object to measure another object. Express the length
as a whole number of length units.

CCMS
1.MD.A.1
1.MD.A.2 **139**

Look at the cubes to measure each item. Write the length.

1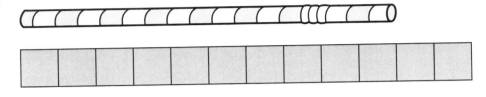

_____ cubes

2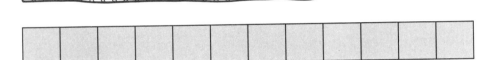

_____ cubes

3

_____ cubes

4

_____ cubes

Cut out the sticks. Use the sticks to measure the trees.

1 About how tall is the **tallest** tree?

_____ sticks tall

2 About how tall is the apple tree?

_____ sticks tall

3 About how tall is the **shortest** tree?

_____ sticks tall

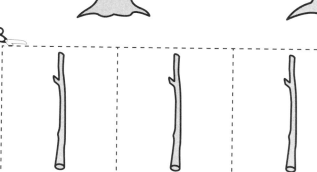

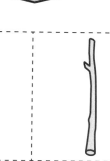

Compare the length of two objects by using a third object.
Use a short object to measure another object. Express the length
as a whole number of length units.

CCMS
1.MD.A.1
1.MD.A.2

141

Read the Problem

Sara used her shoe to measure desks.
Her desk was 5 shoes tall.
Mr. Hall's desk was 4 shoes taller than Sara's desk.
How many shoes tall was Mr. Hall's desk?

Think About It

1 You will find out how many shoes tall _____ was.

   ○ Sara's desk   ○ Mr. Hall   ○ Mr. Hall's desk

2 Mark the number sentence that tells about the problem.

   ○ $5 - 4 = ?$ ○ $5 + 4 = ?$ ○ $5 + 5 = ?$

Solve the Problem

3 Use this work space.

4 Mr. Hall's desk was _____ shoes tall.

Check Your Work

5 Do your answers make sense?   ○ yes   ○ no

CCMS
1.MD.A.1
1.MD.A.2
Compare the length of two objects by using a third object.
Use a short object to measure another object. Express the length
as a whole number of length units.

142

Math Fundamentals • EMC 3081 • © Evan-Moor Corp.

Time

Mathematical Practices in This Unit

Make sense of problems and persevere in solving them: *pages 147, 152*

Reason abstractly and quantitatively: *pages 147, 152*

Construct viable arguments and critique the reasoning of others: *pages 144, 148*

Model with mathematics: *pages 147, 152*

Attend to precision: *pages 147, 152*

Look for and make use of structure: *pages 144, 145, 146, 149, 150, 151*

Math Models

Telling time by the hour

You can measure time using clocks. You can tell and write time in hours.

Analog Clock

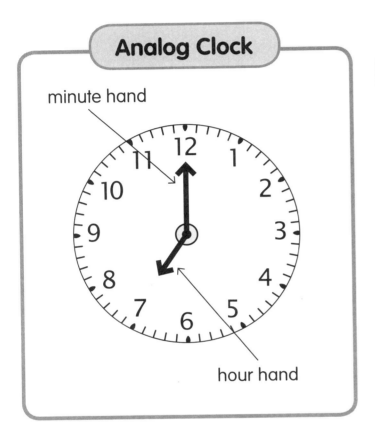

minute hand

hour hand

Digital Clock

hour

minutes

We say the time is **seven o'clock**. We write **7:00**.

Think

One hour = 60 minutes. What time will it be **one hour** after **7:00**?

Look at the time on the analog clock. Draw a line to the digital clock with the same time.

Example

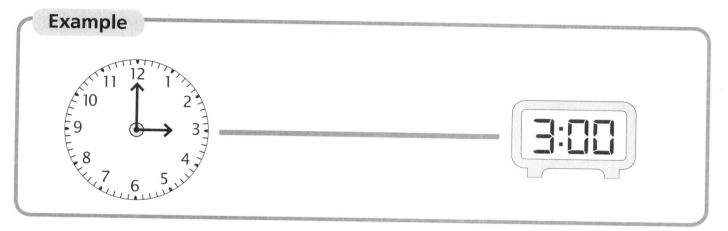

①

②

③

④

⑤

⑥

Look at the time on the analog clock. Write the time on the digital clock.

❶

❸

❷

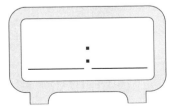

❹

CCMS 1.MD.B.3 Tell and write time in hours using analog and digital clocks.

Math Fundamentals • EMC 3081 • © Evan-Moor Corp.

Read the Problem

The school day ends at 3:00.
A baseball game begins an hour later.
At what time does the game begin?

Think About It

1 You will find out what time _____.

  ○ the school day ends   ○ the game begins

2 To find out the answer, you will _____.

  ○ go ahead one hour   ○ go back one hour

Solve the Problem

3 Use this work space.

4 The game begins at _____:_____.

Check Your Work

5 Do your answers make sense?   ○ yes   ○ no

Math Models

Telling time by the half-hour

You can tell and write time in half-hours.

Analog Clock

hour hand

minute hand

The hour hand is past 7.

The minute hand is 30 minutes past the hour.

Digital Clock

hour

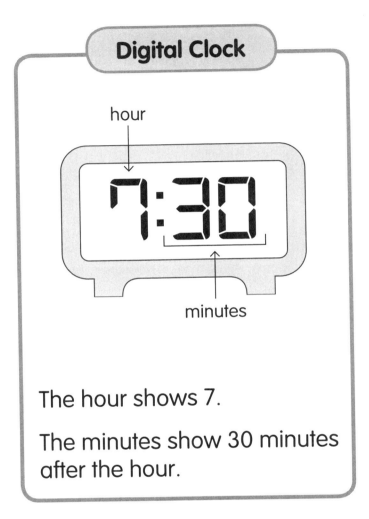

minutes

The hour shows 7.

The minutes show 30 minutes after the hour.

We say the time is **seven thirty** or **half past seven**. We write **7:30**.

Think

What time will it be **30 minutes** after **7:30**?

148 CCMS 1.MD.B.3 Tell and write time in half-hours using analog and digital clocks.

Math Fundamentals • EMC 3081 • © Evan-Moor Corp.

Look at the time on the analog clock. Draw a line to the digital clock with the same time.

Example

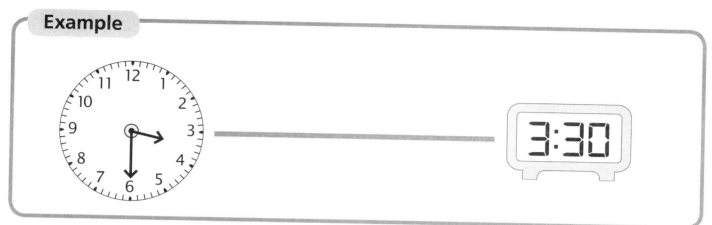

1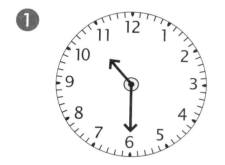

2

3

4

5

6

Tell and write time in half-hours using analog and digital clocks.

Look at the time on the analog clock. Write the time on the digital clock.

①

③

②

④

CCMS
1.MD.B.3
Tell and write time in half-hours using analog and digital clocks.

Math Fundamentals • EMC 3081 • © Evan-Moor Corp.

Fill in the circle below the digital clock that shows the same time as the analog clock.

1

○ ○

3

○ ○

2

○ ○

4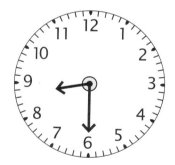

○ ○

Tell and write time in half-hours using analog and digital clocks.

Read the Problem

Jason reads every night at 8:00.
He reads a half-hour before he goes to bed.
At what time does Jason go to bed?

Think About It

1 You will find out what time Jason _____.

○ reads   ○ goes to bed

2 To find the answer, you will _____.

○ go ahead a half-hour   ○ go back a half-hour

Solve the Problem

3 Use this work space.

4 Jason goes to bed at ____:____.

Check Your Work

5 Do your answers make sense?   ○ yes   ○ no

CCMS 1.MD.B.3 Tell and write time in half-hours using analog and digital clocks.

Math Fundamentals • EMC 3081 • © Evan-Moor Corp.

Charts and Graphs

Domain

Measurement and Data

Cluster

Represent and interpret data.

Standard in Cluster

1.MD.C.4 Organize, represent, and interpret data with up to three categories; ask and answer questions about the total number of data points, how many in each category, and how many more or less are in one category than in another.

Mathematical Practices in This Unit

Make sense of problems and persevere in solving them: *pages 158, 162, 166, 170*

Reason abstractly and quantitatively: *pages 154, 155, 156, 157, 158, 159, 160, 161, 162, 163, 164, 165, 166, 167, 168, 169, 170*

Construct viable arguments and critique the reasoning of others: *pages 154, 159, 163, 167*

Model with mathematics: *pages 160, 161, 162, 164, 165, 166, 168, 169, 170*

Attend to precision: *pages 154, 155, 156, 157, 158, 159, 163, 167*

Look for and make use of structure: *pages 154, 155, 156, 157, 158, 159, 163, 167*

Math Models

Understanding charts and graphs

You can use charts and graphs to get meaning from data and answer questions.

Kim and her friends have pets. What kinds of pets do they have? These charts and graphs can show you.

Tally Chart

Our Pets

cats	IIII
dogs	IIII I
birds	II

Picture Graph

Our Pets

cats	🐱 🐱 🐱 🐱 🐱
dogs	🐶 🐶 🐶 🐶 🐶 🐶
birds	🐦 🐦

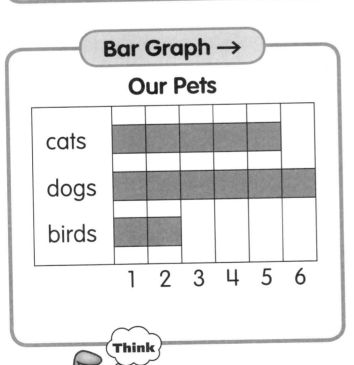

Bar Graph →

Our Pets

Bar Graph ↑

Our Pets

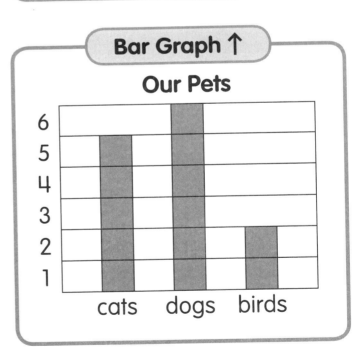

Think

Which type of pet do Kim and her friends have the most of? Explain how each chart and graph shows you.

 CCMS 1.MD.C.4 Interpret data with up to three categories.

Math Fundamentals • EMC 3081 • © Evan-Moor Corp.

Look at the tally chart. Answer the questions.

ⵌ = 5

Our Favorite Lunch	
sandwiches	ⵌ I
pizza	ⵌ II
tacos	ⵌ ⵌ I

1 What is this chart about? _____

_____

2 Which food was picked by the most people?

○ sandwiches   ○ pizza   ○ tacos

3 How many people like sandwiches the best?

_____ people

4 How many more people picked tacos than pizza?

_____ more people picked tacos

Interpret data with up to three categories.

Look at the picture graph. Answer the questions.

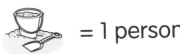 = 1 person

Do you want to go to the beach?		
🪣		
🪣	🪣	
🪣	🪣	🪣
🪣	🪣	🪣
Yes	**No**	**Maybe**

1 What is this picture graph about? _____

_____

2 How many people do **not** want to go?
○ 5 people   ○ 3 people   ○ 2 people

3 How many people answered the question?

_____ people

156 **CCMS 1.MD.C.4** Interpret data with up to three categories.

Math Fundamentals • EMC 3081 • © Evan-Moor Corp.

Look at the bar graph. Answer the questions.

How do you go to school?						
car						
bike						
walk						
	1	2	3	4	5	

1 What is this bar graph about? _____

_____

2 How many more children walk than ride a bike?

_____ more children

3 How do the most children go to school?
   ○ car   ○ bike   ○ walk

4 How many children answered the question?   _____ children

Name _____

Read the Problem and Complete the Graph

Last summer, Kate and her friends made a graph to show when each of them lost a tooth. Look at the graph. Answer the questions.

〰 = 1 tooth

Lost Teeth		
		🦷
		🦷
🦷		🦷
🦷	🦷	🦷
🦷	🦷	🦷
June	**July**	**August**

Think About It

1 What is this graph about?

_____

2 You will look at each _____.
  ○ tally   ○ picture   ○ bar

Interpret the Graph

3 The children lost the most teeth in the month of _____.

4 How many more teeth were lost in August than in June?

_____ more teeth

5 How many teeth were lost in all?   _____ teeth lost in all

Check Your Work

6 Do your answers make sense?   ○ yes   ○ no

You can make a tally chart to show data and answer questions.

Jamie saw 10 blue jays, 2 crows, and 7 robins.
How many of each type of bird did he see?

I wrote one tally mark for each type of bird Jamie saw.

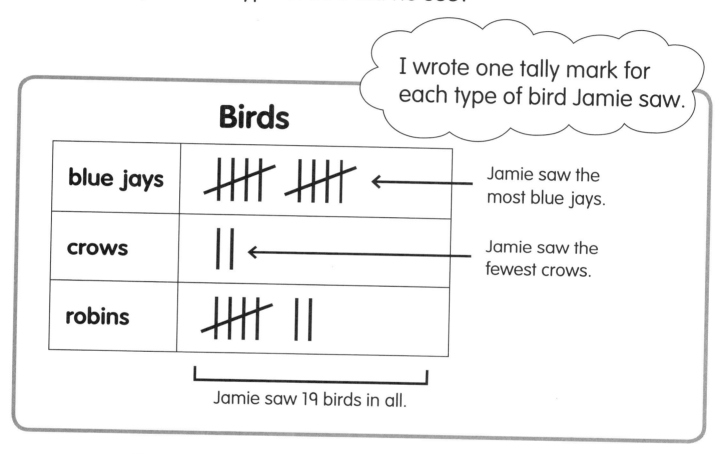

Birds

blue jays	‖‖‖ ‖‖‖	←	Jamie saw the most blue jays.
crows	‖	←	Jamie saw the fewest crows.
robins	‖‖‖ ‖		

Jamie saw 19 birds in all.

Think

How many more blue jays than crows did Jamie see?
Explain your thinking.

Organize, represent, and interpret data with up to three categories.

CCMS
1.MD.C.4

Read the word problem. Use the data to complete the tally chart.
Then answer the questions.

➤ Tim asked some children, "Have you ever been on an airplane?" 6 children said "Yes." 9 children said "No."

$\cancel{||||}$ = 5

1

Have you ever been on an airplane?	
Yes	
No	

2 What is this tally chart about? _____

_____

3 Have most of the children been on a plane?

○ yes   ○ no

4 How many children answered the question? _____ children

 CCMS 1.MD.C.4 Organize, represent, and interpret data with up to three categories.

Math Fundamentals • EMC 3081 • © Evan-Moor Corp.

Read the word problem. Use the data to complete the tally chart.
Then answer the questions.

➤ Mrs. Soto's class voted for the game they like best.
The data shows how the children voted.

$\cancel{||||}$ = 5

1

Use this data:	
soccer	8
baseball	7
4-square	3

Our Favorite Game	
soccer	
baseball	
4-square	

2 Which game got the most votes? _____

3 How many more children chose soccer than 4-square?

_____ more children

4 How many children voted? _____ children

Organize, represent, and interpret data with up to three categories. **CCMS 1.MD.C.4** **161**

Read the Problem and Complete the Chart

1 Read the chart. Look at the total votes for each apple. Write the tally marks to complete the chart. Then answer the questions.

Apples We Like		
Color	Tallies	Total
🍎 red		11
🍏 green		5
🍎 yellow		4

Think About It

2 This chart is about which color apples children like.
○ yes   ○ no

3 You completed the chart with _____.
○ tally marks   ○ pictures   ○ bars

Interpret the Chart

4 The least favorite apple is _____.

5 How many more children voted for red apples than yellow?

_____ more children

6 How many children voted in all?   _____ children

Check Your Work

7 Do your answers make sense?   ○ yes   ○ no

CCMS 1.MD.C.4 Organize, represent, and interpret data with up to three categories.

Math Fundamentals • EMC 3081 • © Evan-Moor Corp.

You can make a picture graph to show data and answer questions.

Dad has a garden. He picked 3 carrots, 12 beans, and 2 radishes.

I drew one picture for each item Dad picked.

What did Dad pick?

carrots	🥕 🥕 🥕
beans	(12 beans)
radishes	(2 radishes)

Dad picked more beans than carrots or radishes.

Dad picked 17 vegetables altogether.

Think

How many fewer carrots than beans did Dad pick? Explain your thinking.

Name _____

Read the word problem. Draw to complete the picture graph.
Then answer the questions.

➤ Keli asked some friends if they like funny or scary movies.
7 friends like funny movies. 3 friends like scary movies.

❶ Write ☺ for what each friend likes.

☺ = 1 friend

Do you like funny or scary movies?	
funny	
scary	

❷ What is this picture graph about? _____

_____

❸ Most of the friends like _____ movies.
   ○ funny   ○ scary

❹ How many friends answered the question?   _____ friends

CCMS 1.MD.C.4   Organize, represent, and interpret data with up to three categories.

Math Fundamentals • EMC 3081 • © Evan-Moor Corp.

Read the word problem. Draw to complete the picture graph.
Then answer the questions.

➤ Each sports team has a different color flag. Players on one team voted for a new flag color. 4 voted for yellow. 6 voted for green. 3 voted for red.

❶ Draw one ⌐ for each vote.

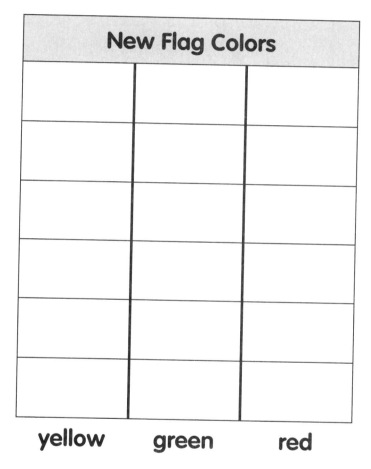

	New Flag Colors	
yellow	green	red

❷ What is this picture graph about? _____

_____

❸ Which flag color got the most votes? _____

Name _____

Read the Problem and Complete the Graph

A family voted for their favorite fruit.

Use this data:

5 voted for bananas

4 voted for plums

3 voted for grapes

❶ Draw ⌒, ◯, and 🍇 to complete the picture graph.

Fruit		
bananas	plums	grapes

Think About It

❷ What is this picture graph about? _____

_____

Interpret the Graph

❸ Which fruit was the favorite of most family members?

_____

❹ How many family members voted? _____ family members

Check Your Work

❺ Do your answers make sense?   ◯ yes   ◯ no

CCMS 1.MD.C.4 Organize, represent, and interpret data with up to three categories.   Math Fundamentals • EMC 3081 • © Evan-Moor Corp.

You can make a bar graph to show data and answer questions.

Marie asked some friends to name their favorite weather.
This is what they said: **sunny 7**
rainy 2
snowy 6

A bar graph uses a shaded bar
to show information.

Our Favorite Weather

I colored one ▮ for each friend's vote.

▮ = 1 person

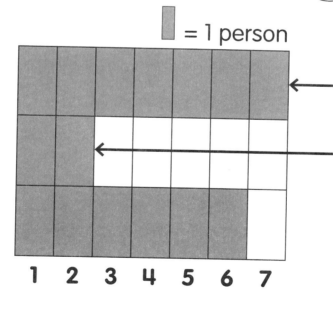

 sunny

rainy

snowy

1 2 3 4 5 6 7

Most of Marie's friends said sunny weather was their favorite.

Fewer people liked rainy than sunny or snowy weather.

15 friends in all named their favorite weather.

Think

How many fewer friends liked rainy weather than sunny weather? Explain your thinking.

Organize, represent, and interpret data with up to three categories.
CCMS 1.MD.C.4 **167**

Read the word problem. Color to complete the bar graph.
Then answer the questions.

➤ Mrs. Garcia asked her students if they like the beach or the forest best. 8 students said they like the beach. 12 students said they like the forest.

1 Color one ▭ to show what each student likes best.

Beach or Forest?

	12		
	11		
	10		
	9		
	8		
	7		
	6		
	5		
	4		
	3		
	2		
	1		

〰️ beach   🌲🌲🌲 forest

2 What is this bar graph about? _____

_____

3 How many more students chose the forest than the beach?

_____ more students

 CCMS 1.MD.C.4   Organize, represent, and interpret data with up to three categories.   Math Fundamentals • EMC 3081 • © Evan-Moor Corp.

Read the word problem. Color to complete the bar graph.
Then answer the questions.

➤ Farmer Tom has hens. Each hen lays one egg every day.
Farmer Tom finds 3 white, 4 brown, and 5 spotted eggs
every day.

① Color one ▮ for
each egg laid.

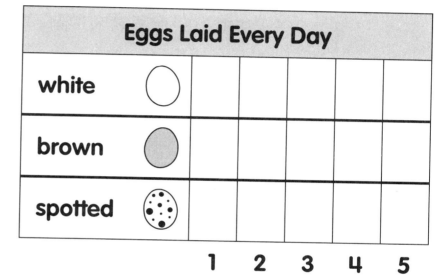

② What is this bar graph about? _____

_____

③ How many fewer white eggs than
spotted eggs are laid each day? _____ fewer white eggs

④ How many eggs are laid each day in all? _____ eggs

Name _____

Read the Problem and Complete the Graph

Mr. Black trains dogs. How many of each size dog does he train?

Use this data:

4 small dogs

7 medium dogs

2 large dogs

Dog Sizes

	7			
	6			
	5			
	4			
	3			
	2			
	1			

small   medium   large

❶ Complete the bar graph.

Think About It

❷ What is this bar graph about?

_____

Interpret the Graph

❸ How many more medium dogs than large dogs does

Mr. Black train?   _____ more medium dogs

❹ How many dogs does he train altogether?   _____ dogs

Check Your Work

❺ Do your answers make sense?   ○ yes   ○ no

 CCMS 1.MD.C.4 Organize, represent, and interpret data with up to three categories.   Math Fundamentals • EMC 3081 • © Evan-Moor Corp.

Money

Skills in Cluster

Apply mathematical process standards to identify coins, their values, and the relationships among them in order to recognize the need for monetary transactions. The student is expected to: (A) identify U.S. coins, including pennies, nickels, dimes, and quarters, by value; (B) write a number with a cent symbol to describe the value of a coin; and (C) use relationships to count by twos, fives, and tens to determine the value of a collection of pennies, nickels, and/or dimes.

> **Note:** While money is not included in the Common Core State Standards at this grade, it provides a valuable real-life context in which to apply other grade-level skills, such as skip counting and adding within 100. Also, some states expect students to learn the value of coins in first grade before solving problems with money in second grade.

Unit Contents

Mathematical Practices in This Unit

Make sense of problems and persevere in solving them: *pages 175, 179, 184*

Reason abstractly and quantitatively: *pages 172, 173, 174, 176, 177, 178, 179, 180, 181, 182, 183, 184*

Construct viable arguments and critique the reasoning of others: *pages 172, 176, 180*

Model with mathematics: *pages 175, 179, 184*

Attend to precision: *pages 172, 175, 176, 179, 180, 184*

Look for and make use of structure: *pages 172, 173, 174, 175, 176, 177, 178, 179, 180, 181, 182, 183, 184*

Math Models

Identifying coins

You can identify pennies, nickels, dimes, and quarters.
Each coin has a different size, look, and value.

What it looks like	What it is called	Its value
	penny	1¢
	nickel	5¢
	dime	10¢
 	quarter	25¢

Think

Look at the chart. Would you rather have
2 quarters or **2 nickels**? Explain your thinking.

Circle the value of each coin.

Examples

5¢

(25¢)

1¢

(10¢)

1

5¢

25¢

4

10¢

1¢

2

25¢

10¢

5

25¢

10¢

3

1¢

5¢

6

5¢

1¢

Draw a line from each coin to its name and/or value.

• dime

• 25¢

• penny

• 5¢

• nickel

• 10¢

Name _____

Read the Problem

Marci has 3 coins.
The values of her coins are 25 cents, 10 cents, and 1 cent.
What are the names of each of Marci's coins?

Think About It

1 You will write the _____ of Marci's coins.

○ value   ○ names   ○ total

Solve the Problem

Use the word box to help you write your answers.

penny   nickel   dime   quarter

2 Marci has a _____, a _____,

and a _____.

Check Your Work

3 Do your answers make sense?   ○ yes   ○ no

Math Models

Writing the value of coins

You can use ¢ to write the value of coins.

Front and Back

   We say, "A penny equals one cent."
We write: **1¢**

   We say, "A nickel equals five cents."
We write: **5¢**

   We say, "A dime equals ten cents."
We write: **10¢**

  We say, "A quarter equals 25 cents."
We write: **25¢**

Think

Why is it important to use ¢ when you write numbers about money? Explain your thinking.

Write the value of each coin.

Examples

5¢

10¢

①

_____

④

_____

②

_____

⑤

_____

③

_____

⑥

_____

Write the value of coins.

Circle the name of each coin. Then write its value.

1

dime

(quarter)

25¢

4

penny

nickel

_____

2

nickel

dime

_____

5

nickel

quarter

_____

3

dime

quarter

_____

6

penny

dime

_____

Name _____

Read the Problem

Jack has a nickel. Teera has a quarter. Mike has a dime. How much money does each child have?

Think About It

1 You will find out how much money _____.

○ in all   ○ each child has   ○ is left

2 Mark the other way to write "cents."

○ $ ○ ?   ○ ¢

Solve the Problem

3 Use this work space.

4 Jack has _____.

5 Teera has _____.

6 Mike has _____.

Check Your Work

7 Do your answers make sense?   ○ yes   ○ no

You can use counting on to find the value of groups of pennies, nickels, and dimes.

You can **count on** for groups of matching coins.
These are some examples:

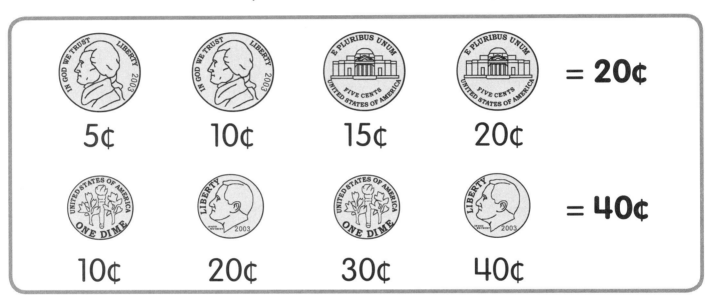

You can **count on** for groups of coins that don't match, too.
Count in order from the largest value to the smallest value coins.

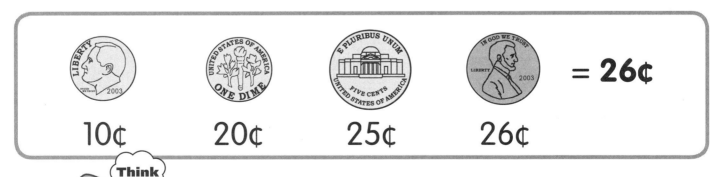

Think

If you had 3 pennies, 1 nickel, and 2 dimes, what order should you use to **count on**? Explain your thinking.

Count on for each group of coins. Write the values.

Examples

  = __15¢__

__5¢__   __10¢__   __15¢__

       = _____

_____   _____   _____   _____   _____   _____

       = _____

_____   _____   _____   _____   _____   _____

     = _____

_____   _____   _____   _____   _____

Count coins.

Count on for each group of coins. Write the values.

        = _____

____ ____ ____ ____

       = _____

____ ____ ____ ____

        = _____

____ ____ ____ ____ ____

       = _____

____ ____ ____ ____

Math Fundamentals • EMC 3081 • © Evan-Moor Corp.

Name _____

Money
Counting coins

7

Count on for each group of coins. Write the value.

1

_____

3

_____

2

_____

4

_____

© Evan-Moor Corp. • EMC 3081 • Math Fundamentals   Count coins.   **183**

Read the Problem

Anna has 2 dimes, 1 nickel, and 3 pennies.
How much money does Anna have?

Think About It

1 You will find out how much money Anna _____.

○ needs   ○ lost   ○ has

2 Write about your plan to solve the problem.

_____

_____

Solve the Problem

3 Use this work space.

4 Anna has _____.

Check Your Work

5 Do your answers make sense?   ○ yes   ○ no

Geometry

Domain

Geometry

Cluster

Reason with shapes and their attributes.

Standards in Cluster

Pathway skill: Identify and describe shapes (squares, circles, triangles, rectangles, hexagons, cubes, cones, cylinders, and spheres).

1.G.A.1 Distinguish between defining attributes (e.g., triangles are closed and three-sided) versus nondefining attributes (e.g., color, orientation, overall size); build and draw shapes to possess defining attributes.

1.G.A.2 Compose two-dimensional shapes (rectangles, squares, trapezoids, triangles, half circles, and quarter circles) or three-dimensional shapes (cubes, right rectangular prisms, right circular cones, and right circular cylinders) to create a composite shape, and compose new shapes from the composite shape.

1.G.A.3 Partition circles and rectangles into two and four equal shares, describe the shares using the words *halves*, *fourths*, and *quarters*, and use the phrases *half of*, *fourth of*, and *quarter of*. Describe the whole as two of, or four of the shares. Understand for these examples that decomposing into more equal shares creates smaller shares.

Unit Contents

Mathematical Practices in This Unit

Make sense of problems and persevere in solving them: *pages 189, 193, 197, 201, 206*

Reason abstractly and quantitatively: *pages 189, 193, 197, 201, 206*

Construct viable arguments and critique the reasoning of others: *pages 186, 190, 194, 197, 198, 202*

Model with mathematics: *pages 189, 193, 201, 206*

Attend to precision: *pages 198, 193, 197, 201, 206*

You can identify two- and three-dimensional shapes.

A **two-dimensional** shape is flat.
These are some examples:

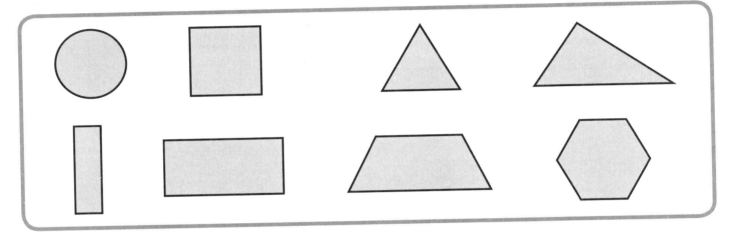

A **three-dimensional shape** has thickness.
These are some examples:

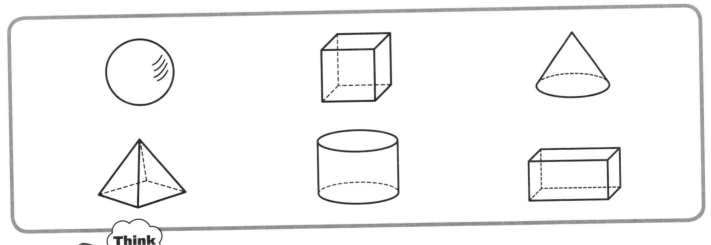

Think

What are some differences between two- and three-dimensional shapes? Explain your thinking.

186 CCMS 1.G.A.1 Identify two- and three-dimensional shapes.

Math Fundamentals • EMC 3081 • © Evan-Moor Corp.

Draw a line from each object to the shape it looks like.

Example

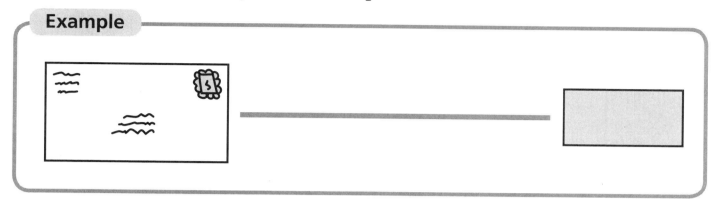

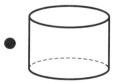

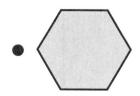

Draw a line from each object to the shape it looks like.

1

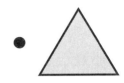

2

3

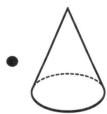

4

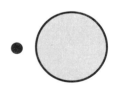

5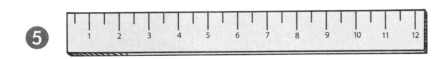

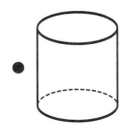

 CCMS 1.G.A.1 Identify two- and three-dimensional shapes.

Math Fundamentals • EMC 3081 • © Evan-Moor Corp.

Read the Problem

Maya and her dad went for a walk to look for shapes.
They saw a house with square windows and a rectangle door.
The house had a triangle tree next to it.
Draw a picture of the house and tree Maya and her dad saw.

Think About It

1 You will draw a house with square windows and a _____ door.
   ○ triangle   ○ square   ○ rectangle

2 You will draw a _____ tree next to the house.
   ○ square   ○ rectangle   ○ triangle

Solve the Problem

3 Draw the house and tree that Maya and her dad saw.

Check Your Work

4 Do your answers make sense?   ○ yes   ○ no

You can identify a shape by looking at what it has.

This is an example:

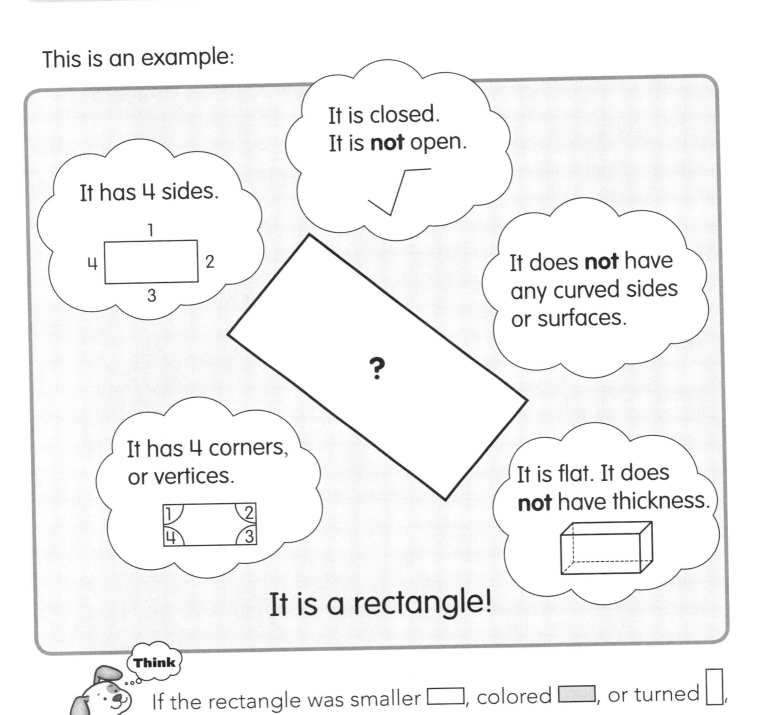

It has 4 sides.

It is closed.
It is **not** open.

It does **not** have any curved sides or surfaces.

It has 4 corners, or vertices.

It is flat. It does **not** have thickness.

It is a rectangle!

Think

If the rectangle was smaller ▭, colored ▬, or turned ▯, would it still be a rectangle? Explain your answer.

190

CCMS
1.G.A.1
1.G.A.2
Distinguish between attributes that compose two- or three-dimensional shapes.

Math Fundamentals • EMC 3081 • © Evan-Moor Corp.

Trace each shape. Write the number of sides and corners.

Example

___3___ sides

___3___ corners

triangle

 3

 3 (square shape)

_____ sides

_____ corners

square

1

_____ sides

_____ corners

rectangle

4

_____ sides

_____ corners

trapezoid

2

_____ sides

_____ corners

triangle

5

_____ sides

_____ corners

rectangle

Distinguish between attributes that compose
two- or three-dimensional shapes.

CCMS
1.G.A.1
1.G.A.2

191

Write the number of flat or curved surfaces for each shape.

1

_____ flat

_____ curved

cone

4

_____ flat

_____ curved

cube

2

_____ flat

_____ curved

sphere

5

_____ flat

_____ curved

cylinder

3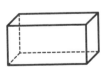

_____ flat

_____ curved

rectangular prism

6

_____ flat

_____ curved

cone

CCMS
1.G.A.1
1.G.A.2
Distinguish between attributes that compose two- or three-dimensional shapes.

Math Fundamentals • EMC 3081 • © Evan-Moor Corp.

Name _____

Read the Problem

Brian has a set of blocks. He can't find one of the blocks. It has 1 flat and 1 curved surface. Circle the missing block.

Think About It

1 You will circle the block that has _____ surface.

○ 1 flat   ○ 1 curved   ○ 1 flat and 1 curved

2 The block will _____.

○ be flat   ○ have thickness   ○ have 4 sides

Solve the Problem

3 Circle the missing block.

Check Your Work

4 Do your answers make sense?   ○ yes   ○ no

© Evan-Moor Corp. • EMC 3081 • Math Fundamentals

Distinguish between attributes that compose
two- or three-dimensional shapes.

CCMS
1.G.A.1
1.G.A.2

193

You can combine shapes to make new shapes.

These are some examples:

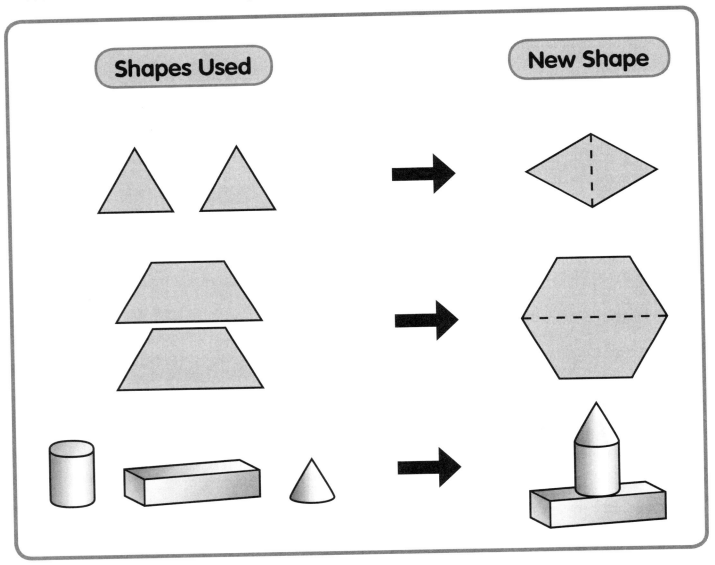

Shapes Used → New Shape

Think

What shapes do you need to build 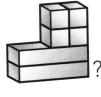?
Explain your thinking.

194

CCMS
1.G.A.2
Compose two-dimensional or three-dimensional shapes
to create composite shapes.

Math Fundamentals • EMC 3081 • © Evan-Moor Corp.

Circle the smaller shapes that can be used to make the bigger shape.

Example

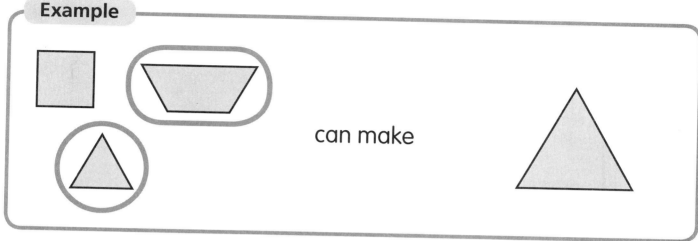

can make

1

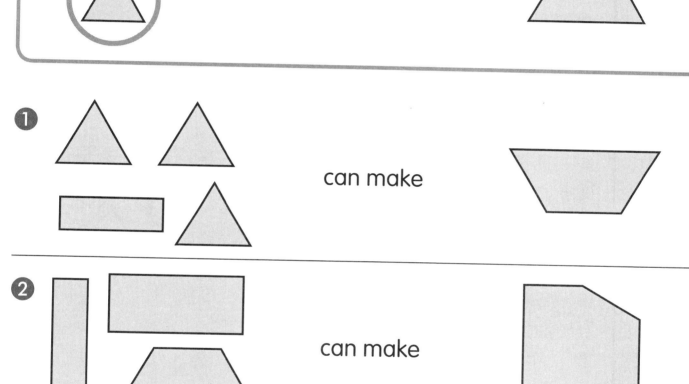

can make

2

can make

3

can make

Compose two-dimensional or three-dimensional shapes to create composite shapes.

CCMS
1.G.A.2   195

Draw a line from each group of shapes to the new shape you can make.

1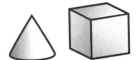

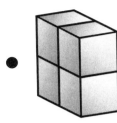

2

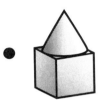

3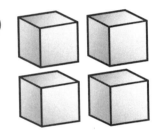

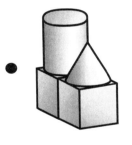

4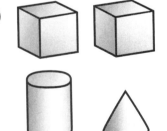

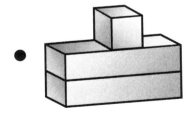

5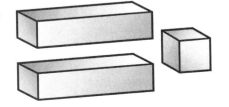

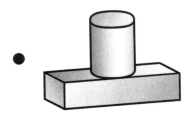

CCMS 1.G.A.2 Compose two-dimensional or three-dimensional shapes to create composite shapes.

Math Fundamentals • EMC 3081 • © Evan-Moor Corp.

Read the Problem

Matt sees 8 ⬜s in the big shape.
Zoey said, "I see more than 8 ⬜s."
How many ⬜s are there?

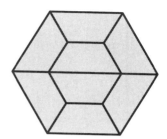

Think About It

❶ You will find out how many _____ compose the big shape.

○ △s   ○ ⬜s   ○ ▱s

❷ Zoey says that there are _____.

○ more than 8   ○ fewer than 8   ○ 8

Solve the Problem

❸ There are _____ ⬜s in the shape.

Check Your Work

❹ Do your answers make sense?   ○ yes   ○ no

Compose two-dimensional or three-dimensional shapes
to create composite shapes.

**CCMS
1.G.A.2** 197

Math Models

Partitioning shapes into equal shares

You can tell if shares, or parts, of a whole are equal or not equal.

These are some examples:

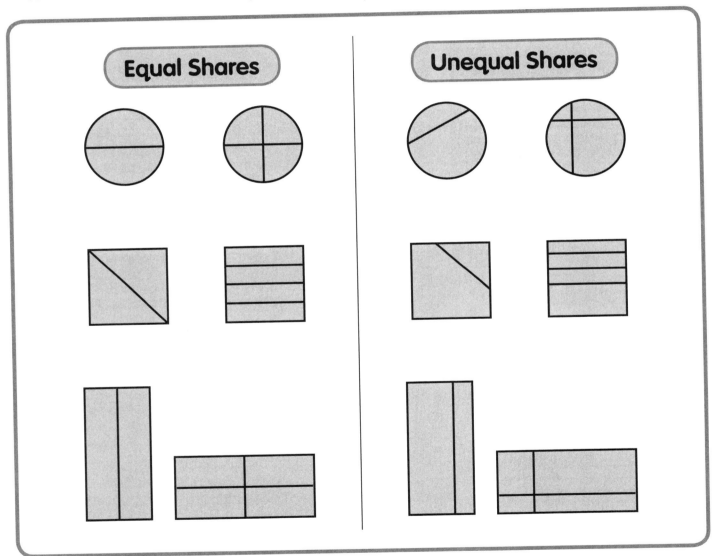

Equal Shares

Unequal Shares

Think

If you are cutting pizza for friends, is it important to cut equal shares? Explain your thinking.

CCMS 1.G.A.3 Partition circles and rectangles into two and four equal shares.

Math Fundamentals • EMC 3081 • © Evan-Moor Corp.

Name _____

Circle 😊 if the shape has **equal** shares, or parts.

Circle 🙁 if the shape has **unequal** shares, or parts.

Examples

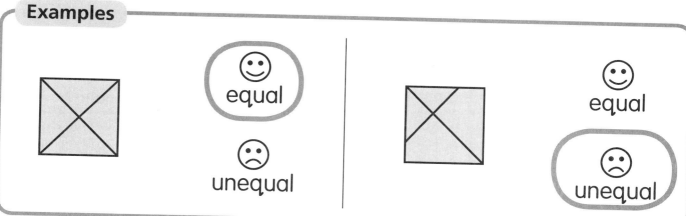

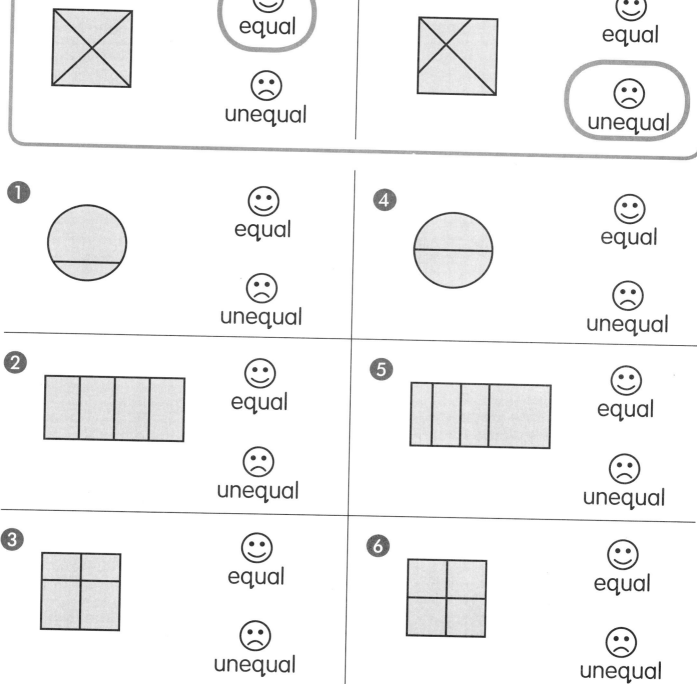

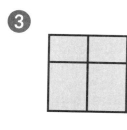

© Evan-Moor Corp. • EMC 3081 • Math Fundamentals

Partition circles and rectangles into two and four equal shares.

CCMS 1.G.A.3 199

Circle the shapes that show **equal** shares, or parts.

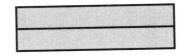

CCMS 1.G.A.3 Partition circles and rectangles into two and four equal shares.

Math Fundamentals • EMC 3081 • © Evan-Moor Corp.

Name _____

Read the Problem

Tami cut a pizza into four equal shares. It looked like this. Circle the shape below that shows one equal share of Tami's pizza.

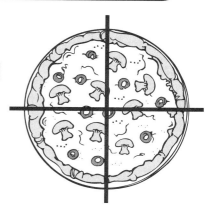

Think About It

1 You will find the shape that is 1 of _____ equal shares.

○ 2   ○ 3   ○ 4

2 A circle has a _____ side.

○ curved   ○ straight   ○ zigzag

Solve the Problem

3 Circle the shape that shows one equal share of Tami's pizza.

Check Your Work

4 Do your answers make sense?   ○ yes   ○ no

Partition circles and rectangles into two and four equal shares.

CCMS
1.G.A.3   201

Math Models

Partitioning shapes into fractional shares

Geometry

> You can show how a fraction is an equal part of a whole shape.

Halves are two equal shares of a whole shape.

Examples

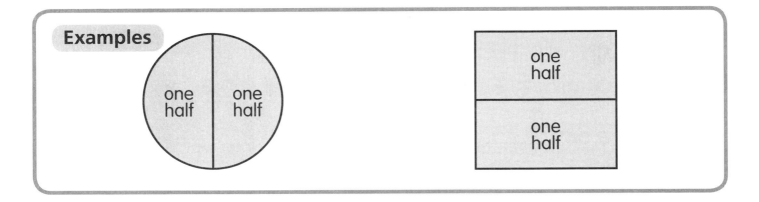

Fourths are four equal shares of a whole shape.
Another name for a fourth is a **quarter**.

Examples

one fourth | one fourth
one fourth | one fourth

one fourth | one fourth
one fourth | one fourth

Think

Which is more, **one half** of a pie or **one fourth** of that pie? Explain your thinking.

CCMS 1.G.A.3 Describe halves and fourths as parts of a whole.

Math Fundamentals • EMC 3081 • © Evan-Moor Corp.

Circle the shape in each row that shows **halves**.

Example

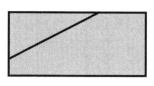 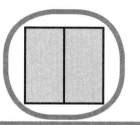

1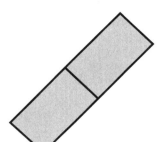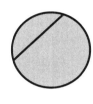

2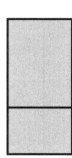

3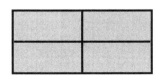

Describe halves and fourths as parts of a whole.

CCMS 1.G.A.3 203

Name _____

Circle the shape in each row that shows **fourths**.

Example

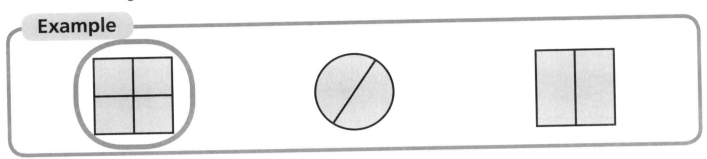

   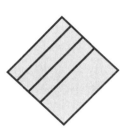

2

3

CCMS 1.G.A.3 Describe halves and fourths as parts of a whole.

Math Fundamentals • EMC 3081 • © Evan-Moor Corp.

Name _____

Circle the name of the shaded part of each shape.

1

whole

half

fourth

2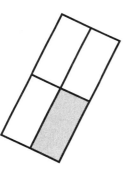

whole

half

fourth

3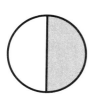

whole

half

fourth

4

whole

half

fourth

5

whole

half

fourth

6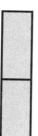

whole

half

fourth

Describe halves and fourths as parts of a whole.

Name _____

Read the Problem

Two friends want to share a square sandwich.
How many ways can it be cut into 2 equal shares?
Draw all the ways in the work space.

Think About It

1 You will find ways to cut a square into _____.

○ halves   ○ fourths   ○ quarters

2 You will _____ the ways.

○ read   ○ draw   ○ cut

Solve the Problem

3 Use this work space.

4 There are _____ ways to cut the sandwich into
2 equal shares.

Check Your Work

5 Do your answers make sense?   ○ yes   ○ no

**CCMS
1.G.A.3** Describe halves and fourths as parts of a whole.

Math Fundamentals • EMC 3081 • © Evan-Moor Corp.

Answer Key

Page 13

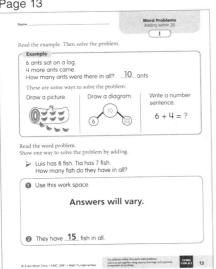

Word Problems
Adding within 20

1

Read the example. Then solve the problem.

Example

6 ants sat on a log.
4 more ants came.
How many ants were there in all? __10__ ants

These are some ways to solve the problem:

Draw a picture.	Draw a diagram.	Write a number sentence.
	10 / 6 / 4	6 + 4 = ?

Read the word problem.
Show one way to solve the problem by adding.

➤ Luis has 8 fish. Tia has 7 fish.
How many fish do they have in all?

① Use this work space.

Answers will vary.

② They have __15__ fish in all.

Page 14

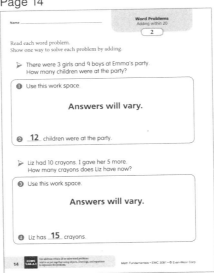

Word Problems
Adding within 20

2

Read each word problem.
Show one way to solve each problem by adding.

➤ There were 3 girls and 9 boys at Emma's party.
How many children were at the party?

① Use this work space.

Answers will vary.

② __12__ children were at the party.

➤ Liz had 10 crayons. I gave her 5 more.
How many crayons does Liz have now?

③ Use this work space.

Answers will vary.

④ Liz has __15__ crayons.

Page 15

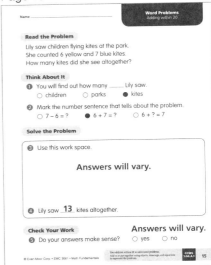

Word Problems
Adding within 20

Read the Problem

Lily saw children flying kites at the park.
She counted 6 yellow and 7 blue kites.
How many kites did she see altogether?

Think About It

① You will find out how many _____ Lily saw.
  ○ children   ○ parks   ● kites

② Mark the number sentence that tells about the problem.
  ○ 7 − 6 = ?   ● 6 + 7 = ?   ○ 6 + ? = 7

Solve the Problem

③ Use this work space.

Answers will vary.

④ Lily saw __13__ kites altogether.

Check Your Work   **Answers will vary.**

⑤ Do your answers make sense?   ○ yes   ○ no

Page 17

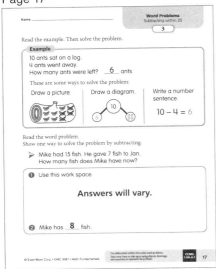

Word Problems
Subtracting within 20

3

Read the example. Then solve the problem.

Example

10 ants sat on a log.
4 ants went away.
How many ants were left? __6__ ants

These are some ways to solve the problem:

Draw a picture.	Draw a diagram.	Write a number sentence.
	10 / 6 / 4	10 − 4 = 6

Read the word problem.
Show one way to solve the problem by subtracting.

➤ Mike had 15 fish. He gave 7 fish to Jan.
How many fish does Mike have now?

① Use this work space.

Answers will vary.

② Mike has __8__ fish.

Page 18

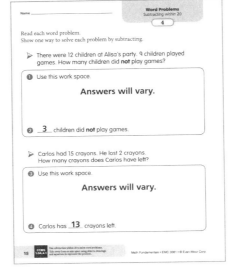

Word Problems
Subtracting within 20

4

Read each word problem.
Show one way to solve each problem by subtracting.

➤ There were 12 children at Alisa's party. 9 children played
games. How many children did **not** play games?

① Use this work space.

Answers will vary.

② __3__ children did **not** play games.

➤ Carlos had 15 crayons. He lost 2 crayons.
How many crayons does Carlos have left?

③ Use this work space.

Answers will vary.

④ Carlos has __13__ crayons left.

Page 19

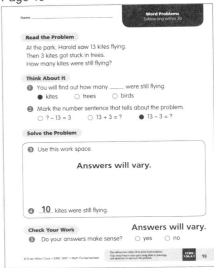

Word Problems
Subtracting within 20

Read the Problem

At the park, Harold saw 13 kites flying.
Then 3 kites got stuck in trees.
How many kites were still flying?

Think About It

① You will find out how many _____ were still flying.
  ● kites   ○ trees   ○ birds

② Mark the number sentence that tells about the problem.
  ○ ? − 13 = 3   ○ 13 + 3 = ?   ● 13 − 3 = ?

Solve the Problem

③ Use this work space.

Answers will vary.

④ __10__ kites were still flying.

Check Your Work   **Answers will vary.**

⑤ Do your answers make sense?   ○ yes   ○ no

Page 21

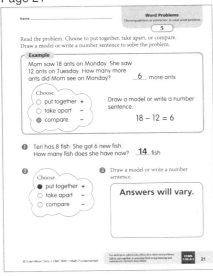

Word Problems
Choosing addition or subtraction to solve word problems

5

Read the problem. Choose to put together, take apart, or compare.
Draw a model or write a number sentence to solve the problem.

Example

Mom saw 18 ants on Monday. She saw
12 ants on Tuesday. How many more
ants did Mom see on Monday? __6__ more ants

Choose.
○ put together +
○ take apart −
● compare

Draw a model or write a number
sentence.
18 − 12 = 6

① Teri has 8 fish. She got 6 new fish.
How many fish does she have now? __14__ fish

② Choose.
● put together +
○ take apart −
○ compare

③ Draw a model or write a number
sentence.

Answers will vary.

Page 22

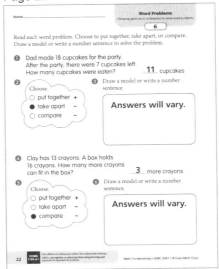

Word Problems
Choosing addition or subtraction to solve word problems

6

Read each word problem. Choose to put together, take apart, or compare.
Draw a model or write a number sentence to solve the problem.

① Dad made 18 cupcakes for the party.
After the party, there were 7 cupcakes left.
How many cupcakes were eaten? __11__ cupcakes

② Choose.
○ put together +
● take apart −
○ compare

③ Draw a model or write a number
sentence.

Answers will vary.

④ Clay has 13 crayons. A box holds
16 crayons. How many more crayons
can fit in the box? __3__ more crayons

⑤ Choose.
○ put together +
○ take apart −
● compare

⑥ Draw a model or write a number
sentence.

Answers will vary.

Page 23

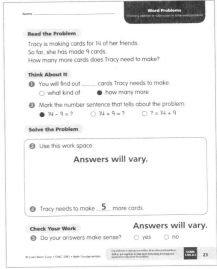

Word Problems
Choosing addition or subtraction to solve word problems

Read the Problem

Tracy is making cards for 14 of her friends.
So far, she has made 9 cards.
How many more cards does Tracy need to make?

Think About It

① You will find out _____ cards Tracy needs to make.
  ○ what kind of   ● how many more

② Mark the number sentence that tells about the problem.
  ● 14 − 9 = ?   ○ 14 + 9 = ?   ○ ? = 14 + 9

Solve the Problem

③ Use this work space.

Answers will vary.

④ Tracy needs to make __5__ more cards.

Check Your Work   **Answers will vary.**

⑤ Do your answers make sense?   ○ yes   ○ no

Page 25

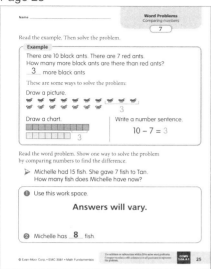

Page 26

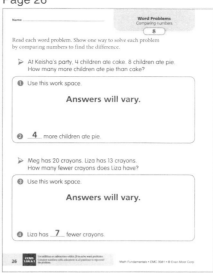

Page 27

Page 29

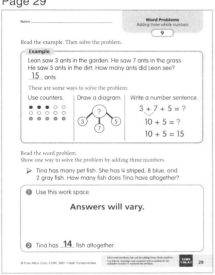

Page 30

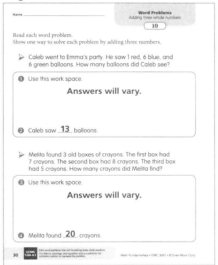

Page 31

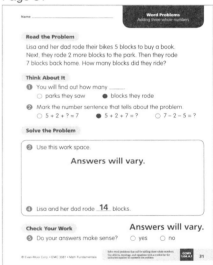

Page 33

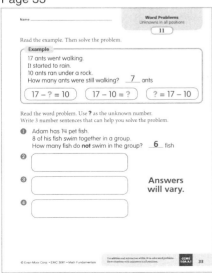

Page 34

Page 35

Page 36

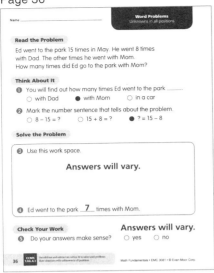

Word Problems
Unknowns in all positions

Read the Problem

Ed went to the park 15 times in May. He went 8 times with Dad. The other times he went with Mom. How many times did Ed go to the park with Mom?

Think About It

❶ You will find out how many times Ed went to the park _____
○ with Dad   ● with Mom   ○ in a car

❷ Mark the number sentence that tells about the problem.
○ 8 − 15 = ?   ○ 15 + 8 = ?   ● ? = 15 − 8

Solve the Problem

❸ Use this work space.

Answers will vary.

❹ Ed went to the park **7** times with Mom.

Check Your Work   **Answers will vary.**

❺ Do your answers make sense?   ○ yes   ○ no

Page 39

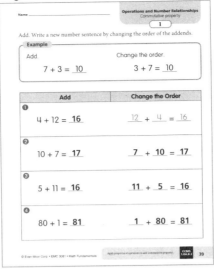

Operations and Number Relationships
Commutative property
1

Add. Write a new number sentence by changing the order of the addends.

Example

Add.	Change the order.
7 + 3 = **10**	3 + 7 = **10**

Add	Change the Order
❶ 4 + 12 = **16**	**12** + **4** = **16**
❷ 10 + 7 = **17**	**7** + **10** = **17**
❸ 5 + 11 = **16**	**11** + **5** = **16**
❹ 80 + 1 = **81**	**1** + **80** = **81**

Page 40

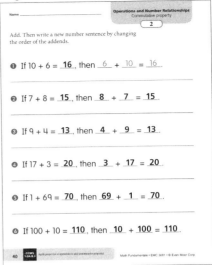

Operations and Number Relationships
Commutative property
2

Add. Then write a new number sentence by changing the order of the addends.

❶ If 10 + 6 = **16**, then **6** + **10** = **16**.

❷ If 7 + 8 = **15**, then **8** + **7** = **15**.

❸ If 9 + 4 = **13**, then **4** + **9** = **13**.

❹ If 17 + 3 = **20**, then **3** + **17** = **20**.

❺ If 1 + 69 = **70**, then **69** + **1** = **70**.

❻ If 100 + 10 = **110**, then **10** + **100** = **110**.

Page 41

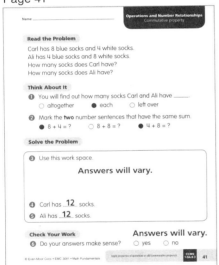

Operations and Number Relationships
Commutative property

Read the Problem

Carl has 8 blue socks and 4 white socks. Ali has 4 blue socks and 8 white socks. How many socks does Carl have? How many socks does Ali have?

Think About It

❶ You will find out how many socks Carl and Ali have _____
○ altogether   ● each   ○ left over

❷ Mark the **two** number sentences that have the same sum.
● 8 + 4 = ?   ○ 8 + 8 = ?   ● 4 + 8 = ?

Solve the Problem

❸ Use this work space.

Answers will vary.

❹ Carl has **12** socks.
❺ Ali has **12** socks.

Check Your Work   **Answers will vary.**

❻ Do your answers make sense?   ○ yes   ○ no

Page 43

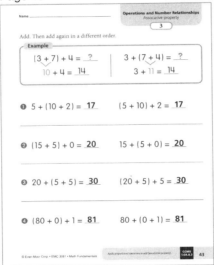

Operations and Number Relationships
Associative property
3

Add. Then add again in a different order.

Example

(3 + 7) + 4 = **?**	3 + (7 + 4) = **?**
10 + 4 = **14**	3 + 11 = **14**

❶ 5 + (10 + 2) = **17**   (5 + 10) + 2 = **17**

❷ (15 + 5) + 0 = **20**   15 + (5 + 0) = **20**

❸ 20 + (5 + 5) = **30**   (20 + 5) + 5 = **30**

❹ (80 + 0) + 1 = **81**   80 + (0 + 1) = **81**

Page 44

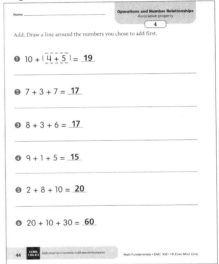

Operations and Number Relationships
Associative property
4

Add. Draw a line around the numbers you chose to add first.

❶ 10 + [4 + 5] = **19**

❷ 7 + 3 + 7 = **17**

❸ 8 + 3 + 6 = **17**

❹ 9 + 1 + 5 = **15**

❺ 2 + 8 + 10 = **20**

❻ 20 + 10 + 30 = **60**

Page 45

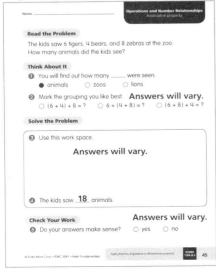

Operations and Number Relationships
Associative property

Read the Problem

The kids saw 6 tigers, 4 bears, and 8 zebras at the zoo. How many animals did the kids see?

Think About It

❶ You will find out how many _____ were seen.
● animals   ○ zoos   ○ lions

❷ Mark the grouping you like best.   **Answers will vary.**
○ (6 + 4) + 8 = ?   ○ 6 + (4 + 8) = ?   ○ (6 + 8) + 4 = ?

Solve the Problem

❸ Use this work space.

Answers will vary.

❹ The kids saw **18** animals.

Check Your Work   **Answers will vary.**

❺ Do your answers make sense?   ○ yes   ○ no

Page 47

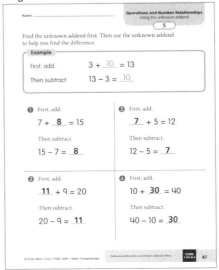

Operations and Number Relationships
Using the unknown addend
5

Find the unknown addend first. Then use the unknown addend to help you find the difference.

Example

First, add.   3 + **10** = 13
Then subtract. 13 − 3 = **10**

❶ First, add.
7 + **8** = 15
Then subtract.
15 − 7 = **8**

❷ First, add.
11 + 9 = 20
Then subtract.
20 − 9 = **11**

❸ First, add.
7 + 5 = 12
Then subtract.
12 − 5 = **7**

❹ First, add.
10 + **30** = 40
Then subtract.
40 − 10 = **30**

Page 48

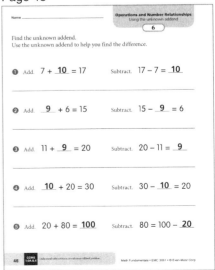

Operations and Number Relationships
Using the unknown addend
6

Find the unknown addend.
Use the unknown addend to help you find the difference.

❶ Add. 7 + **10** = 17   Subtract. 17 − 7 = **10**

❷ Add. **9** + 6 = 15   Subtract. 15 − **9** = 6

❸ Add. 11 + **9** = 20   Subtract. 20 − 11 = **9**

❹ Add. **10** + 20 = 30   Subtract. 30 − **10** = 20

❺ Add. 20 + 80 = **100**   Subtract. 80 = 100 − **20**

Page 49

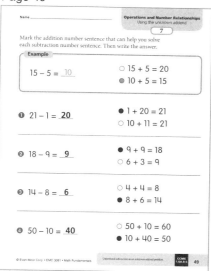

Page 50

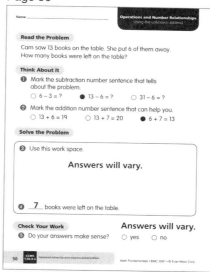

Page 53

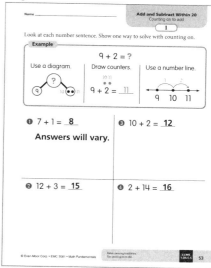

Page 54

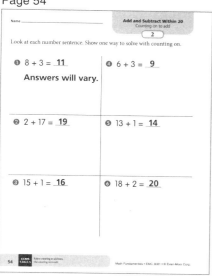

Page 55

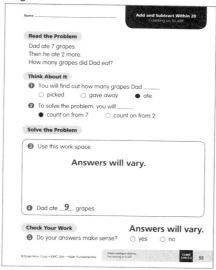

Page 57

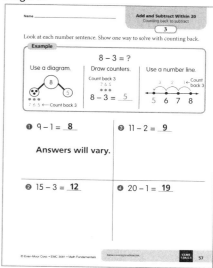

Page 58

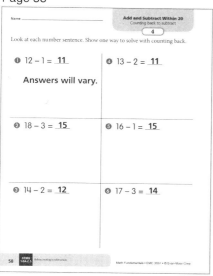

Page 59

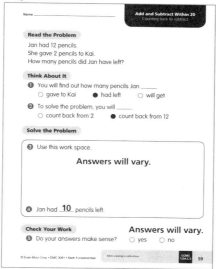

Page 61

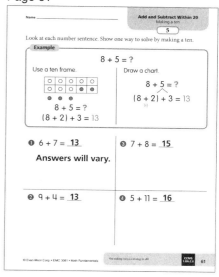

Page 62

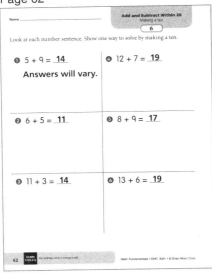

Name _____

Add and Subtract Within 20
Making a ten
6

Look at each number sentence. Show one way to solve by making a ten.

❶ 5 + 9 = **14**   ❹ 12 + 7 = **19**

Answers will vary.

❷ 6 + 5 = **11**   ❺ 8 + 9 = **17**

❸ 11 + 3 = **14**   ❻ 13 + 6 = **19**

Page 63

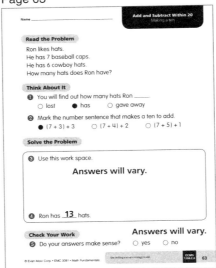

Name _____

Add and Subtract Within 20
Making a ten

Read the Problem

Ron likes hats.
He has 7 baseball caps.
He has 6 cowboy hats.
How many hats does Ron have?

Think About It

❶ You will find out how many hats Ron _____.
  ○ lost   ● has   ○ gave away

❷ Mark the number sentence that makes a ten to add.
  ● (7 + 3) + 3   ○ (7 + 4) + 2   ○ (7 + 5) + 1

Solve the Problem

❸ Use this work space.
  Answers will vary.

❹ Ron has **13** hats.

Check Your Work   **Answers will vary.**
❺ Do your answers make sense?   ○ yes   ○ no

Page 65

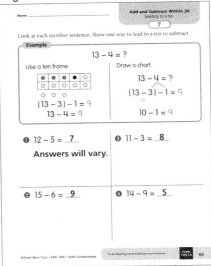

Name _____

Add and Subtract Within 20
Leading to a ten
7

Look at each number sentence. Show one way to lead to a ten to subtract.

Example

13 − 4 = ?

Use a ten frame.	Draw a chart.
	13 − 4 = ?
	(13 − 3) − 1 = 9
(13 − 3) − 1 = 9	
13 − 4 = 9	10 − 1 = 9

❶ 12 − 5 = **7**   ❸ 11 − 3 = **8**

Answers will vary.

❷ 15 − 6 = **9**   ❹ 14 − 9 = **5**

Page 66

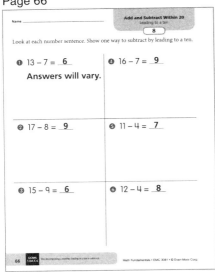

Name _____

Add and Subtract Within 20
Leading to a ten
8

Look at each number sentence. Show one way to subtract by leading to a ten.

❶ 13 − 7 = **6**   ❹ 16 − 7 = **9**

Answers will vary.

❷ 17 − 8 = **9**   ❺ 11 − 4 = **7**

❸ 15 − 9 = **6**   ❻ 12 − 4 = **8**

Page 67

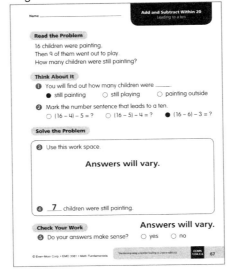

Name _____

Add and Subtract Within 20
Leading to a ten

Read the Problem

16 children were painting.
Then 9 of them went out to play.
How many children were still painting?

Think About It

❶ You will find out how many children were _____.
  ● still painting   ○ still playing   ○ painting outside

❷ Mark the number sentence that leads to a ten.
  ○ (16 − 4) − 5 = ?   ○ (16 − 5) − 4 = ?   ● (16 − 6) − 3 = ?

Solve the Problem

❸ Use this work space.
  Answers will vary.

❹ **7** children were still painting.

Check Your Work   **Answers will vary.**
❺ Do your answers make sense?   ○ yes   ○ no

Page 69

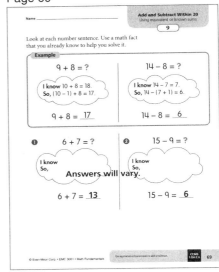

Name _____

Add and Subtract Within 20
Using equivalent or known sums
9

Look at each number sentence. Use a math fact
that you already know to help you solve it.

Example

9 + 8 = ?	14 − 8 = ?
I know 10 + 8 = 18. So, (10 − 1) + 8 = 17.	I know 14 − 7 = 7. So, 14 − (7 + 1) = 6.
9 + 8 = **17**	14 − 8 = **6**

❶ 6 + 7 = ?   ❷ 15 − 9 = ?

I know   I know
So,   So,
Answers will vary.

6 + 7 = **13**   15 − 9 = **6**

Page 70

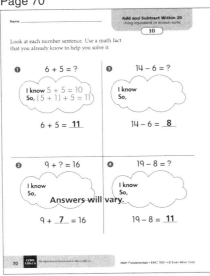

Name _____

Add and Subtract Within 20
Using equivalent or known sums
10

Look at each number sentence. Use a math fact
that you already know to help you solve it.

❶ 6 + 5 = ?   ❸ 14 − 6 = ?

I know 5 + 5 = 10   I know
So, (5 + 1) + 5 = 11   So,

6 + 5 = **11**   14 − 6 = **8**

❷ 9 + ? = 16   ❹ 19 − 8 = ?

I know   I know
So,   So,
Answers will vary.

9 + **7** = 16   19 − 8 = **11**

Page 71

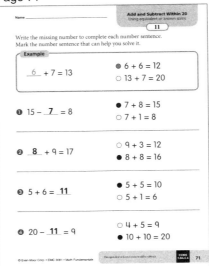

Name _____

Add and Subtract Within 20
Using equivalent or known sums
11

Write the missing number to complete each number sentence.
Mark the number sentence that can help you solve it.

Example

6 + 7 = 13
  ● 6 + 6 = 12
  ○ 13 + 7 = 20

❶ 15 − **7** = 8
  ● 7 + 8 = 15
  ○ 7 + 1 = 8

❷ **8** + 9 = 17
  ○ 9 + 3 = 12
  ● 8 + 8 = 16

❸ 5 + 6 = **11**
  ● 5 + 5 = 10
  ○ 5 + 1 = 6

❹ 20 − **11** = 9
  ○ 4 + 5 = 9
  ● 10 + 10 = 20

Page 72

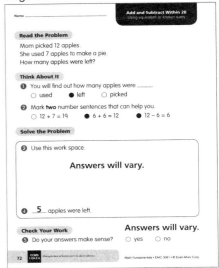

Name _____

Add and Subtract Within 20
Using equivalent or known sums

Read the Problem

Mom picked 12 apples.
She used 7 apples to make a pie.
How many apples were left?

Think About It

❶ You will find out how many apples were _____.
  ○ used   ● left   ○ picked

❷ Mark **two** number sentences that can help you.
  ○ 12 + 7 = 19   ● 6 + 6 = 12   ● 12 − 6 = 6

Solve the Problem

❸ Use this work space.
  Answers will vary.

❹ **5** apples were left.

Check Your Work   **Answers will vary.**
❺ Do your answers make sense?   ○ yes   ○ no

Page 75

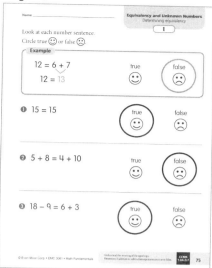

Page 76

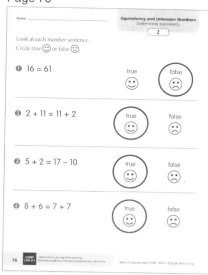

Page 77

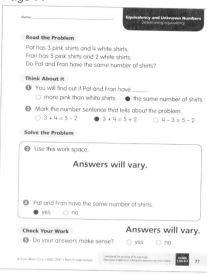

Page 79

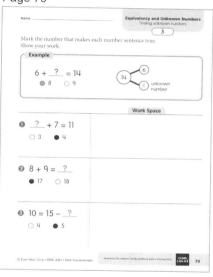

Page 80

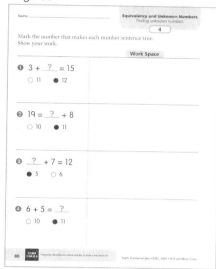

Page 81

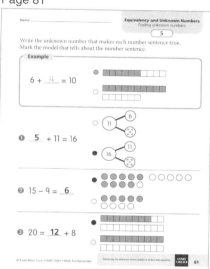

Page 82

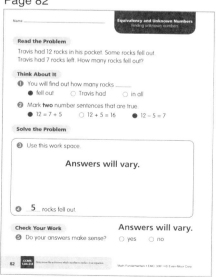

Page 85

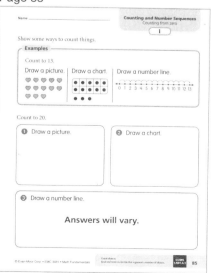

Page 86

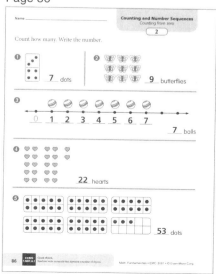

Page 87

Page 88

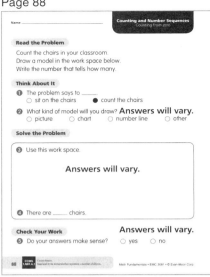

Page 90

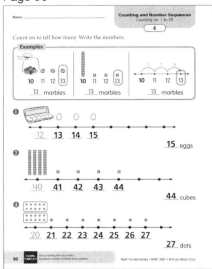

Page 91

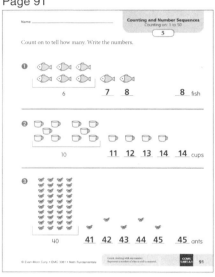

Page 92

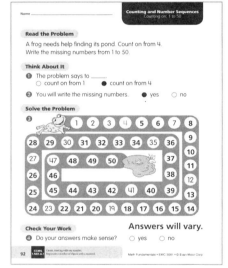

Page 94

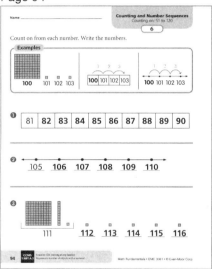

Page 95

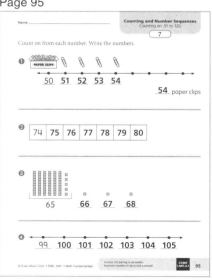

Page 96

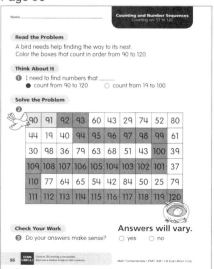

Page 98

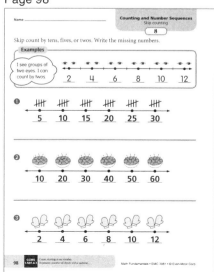

Page 99

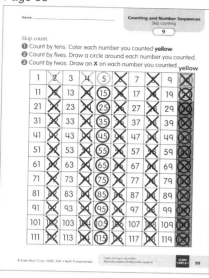

Page 100

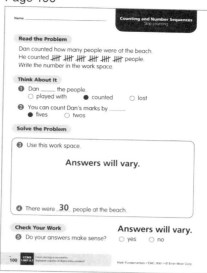

Page 102

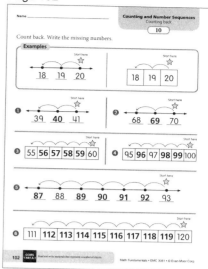

Page 103

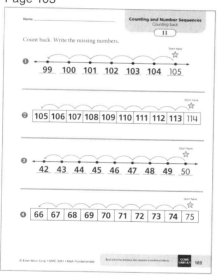

Page 104

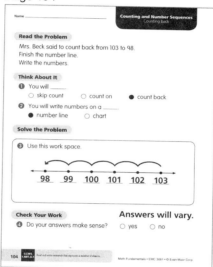

Page 107

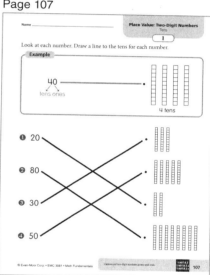

Page 108

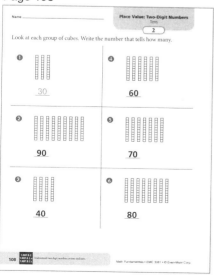

Page 109

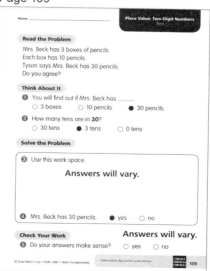

Page 111

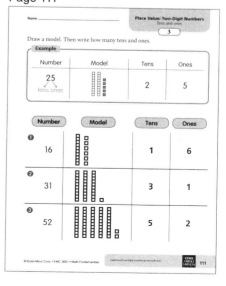

Page 112

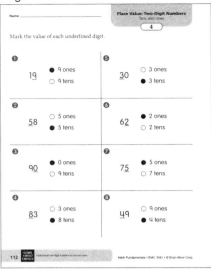

Page 113

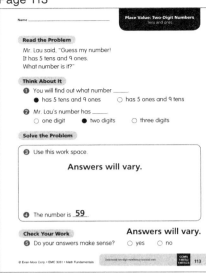

Page 115

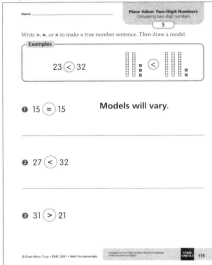

Page 116

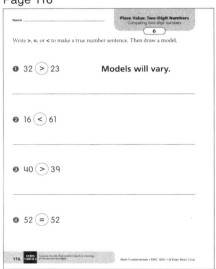

Page 117

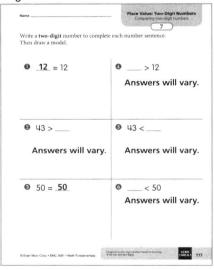

Page 118

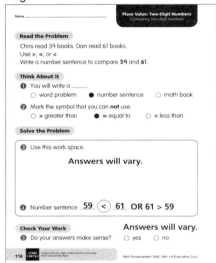

Page 121

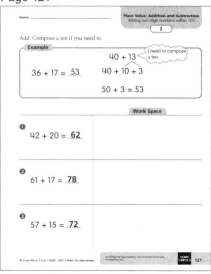

Page 122

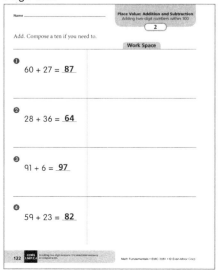

Page 123

Page 125

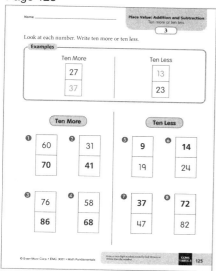

Page 126

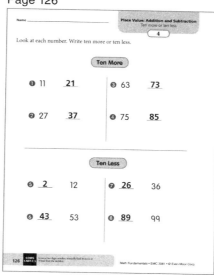

Page 127

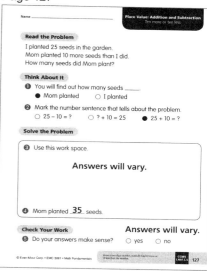

Page 129

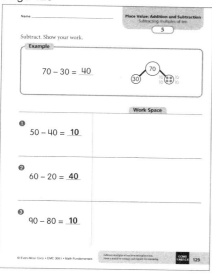

Page 130

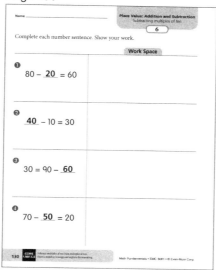

Page 131

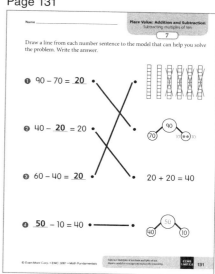

Page 132

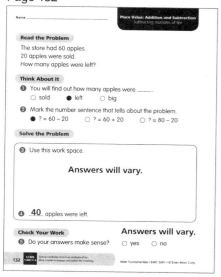

Page 135

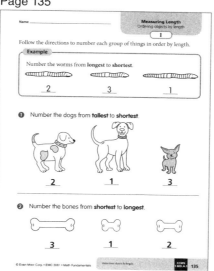

Page 136

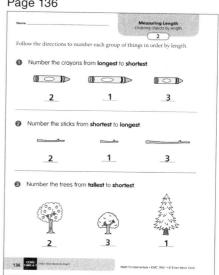

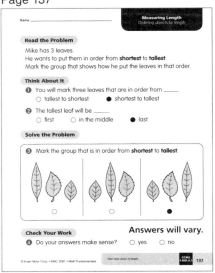

Page 137

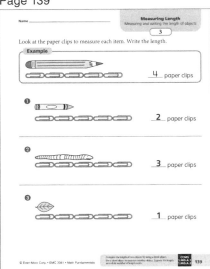

Page 139

Page 140

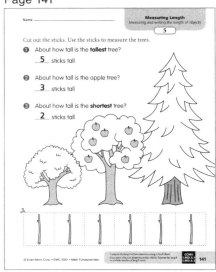

Page 141

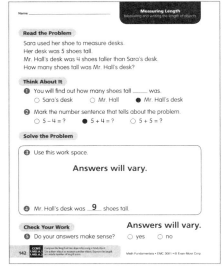

Page 142

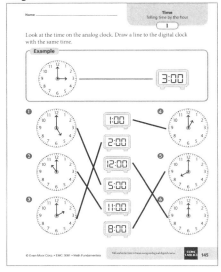

Page 145

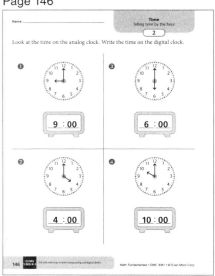

Page 146

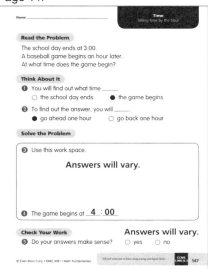

Page 147

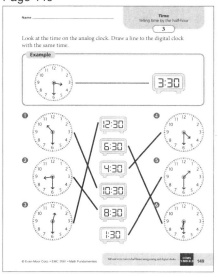

Page 149

Page 150

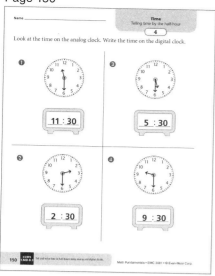

Page 151

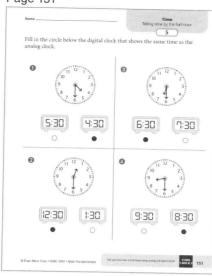

Page 152

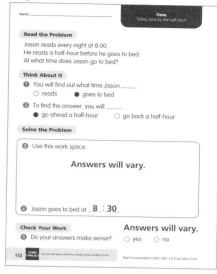

Page 155

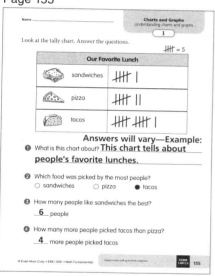

Page 156

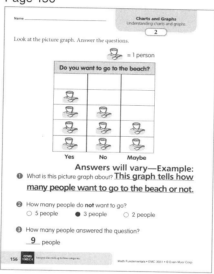

Page 157

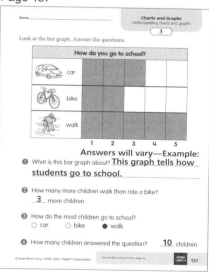

Page 158

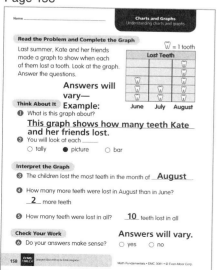

Page 160

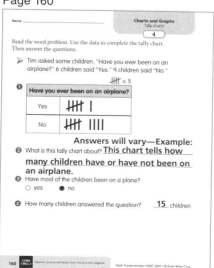

Page 161

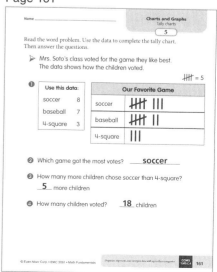

Page 162

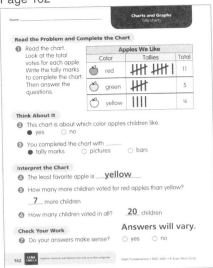

Page 164

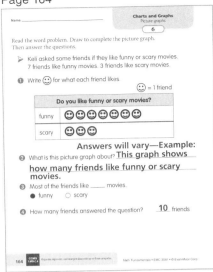

Page 165

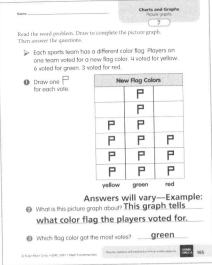

Page 166

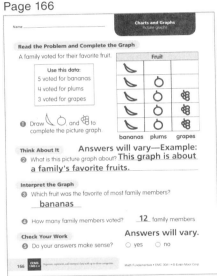

Page 168

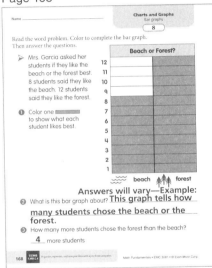

Page 169

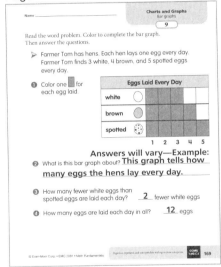

Page 170

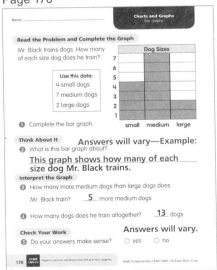

Page 173

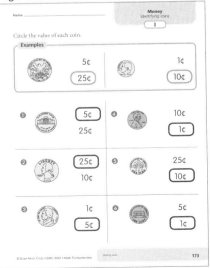

Page 174

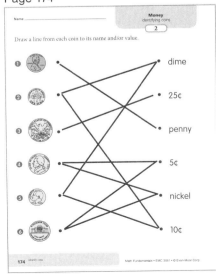

Page 175

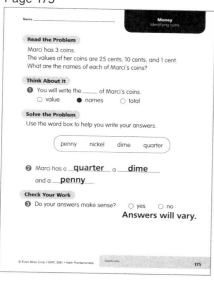

Page 177

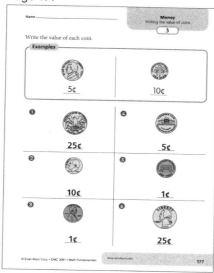

Page 178

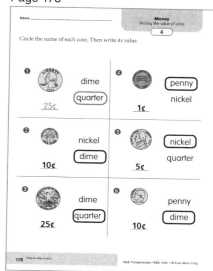

Page 179

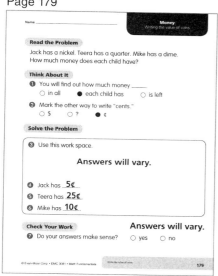

Page 181

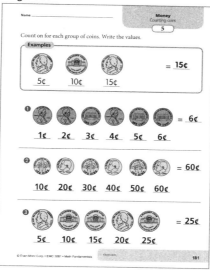

Page 182

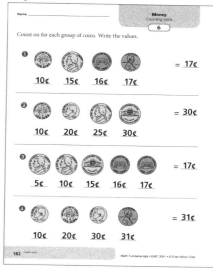

Page 183

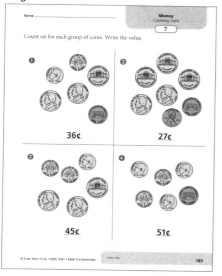

Page 184

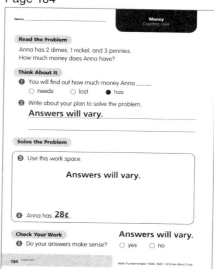

Page 187

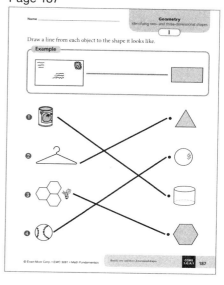

© Evan-Moor Corp. • EMC 3081 • Math Fundamentals

221

Page 188

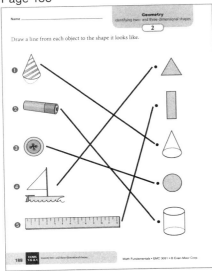

Page 189

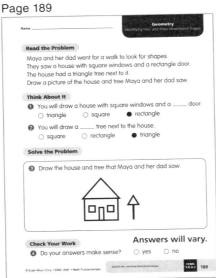

Page 191

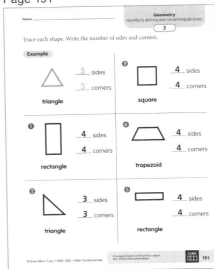

Page 192

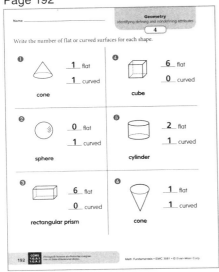

Page 193

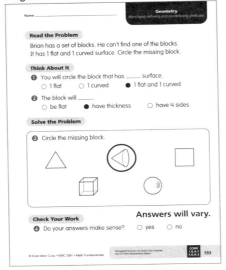

Page 195

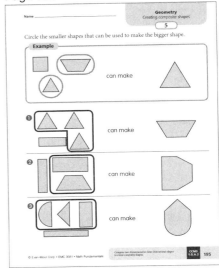

Page 196

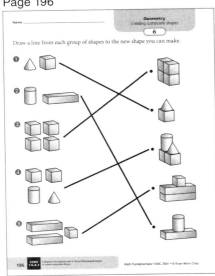

Page 197

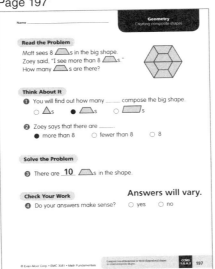

Page 199

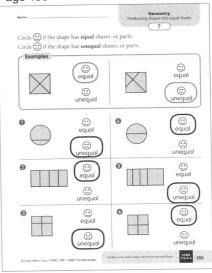

Page 200

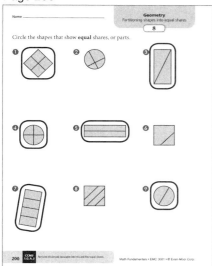

Page 201

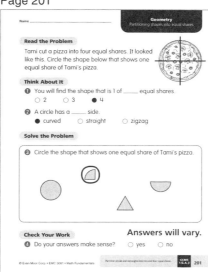

Page 203

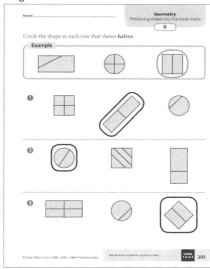

Page 204

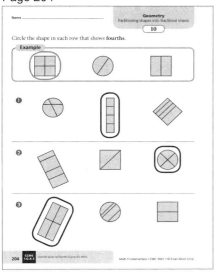

Page 205

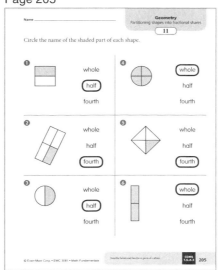

Page 206

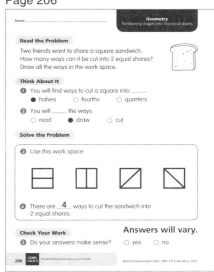

Daily Word Problems

Grades 1–6

Daily Word Problems is the perfect resource to improve students' problem-solving skills. The all-new word problems are written to support current math standards and provide consistent spiral review of math concepts.

- 36 weeks of activities give practice of grade-level math concepts such as addition, multiplication, fractions, logic, algebra, and more.

- Monday through Thursday's activities present a one- or two-step word problem, while Friday's format is more extensive and requires multiple steps.

- The multi-step problems require students to incorporate **higher-order thinking skills.**

128 pages. Correlated to current standards.
www.evan-moor.com/dwp

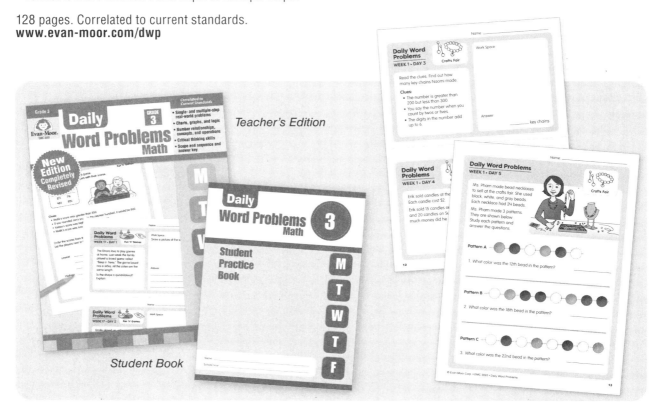

Teacher's Edition

Student Book

Order the format right for you

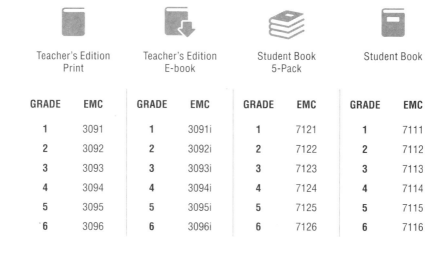

Teacher's Edition Print		Teacher's Edition E-book		Student Book 5-Pack		Student Book	
GRADE	EMC	GRADE	EMC	GRADE	EMC	GRADE	EMC
1	3091	1	3091i	1	7121	1	7111
2	3092	2	3092i	2	7122	2	7112
3	3093	3	3093i	3	7123	3	7113
4	3094	4	3094i	4	7124	4	7114
5	3095	5	3095i	5	7125	5	7115
6	3096	6	3096i	6	7126	6	7116